N.K. Sondhi

N.K. Sondhi's first book was *Management of Banking*, which draws upon his experiences as a manager in the Punjab National Bank. He then turned to fiction writing, bringing forth the seen and unseen aftermaths of the partition of India in 1947 in his novel *Cart full of Husk*. He followed it up with a short non-fiction, *Forgotten City of Delhi (How Delhi became Delhi)*. He wrote his next book, *A Match Made in Heaven: A 2000-year-old love story*, based on the life of an Indian princess, who became first queen of Korea in 48 AD.

Working with young people as he pursued social activities after his retirement, he sensed the restlessness among youngsters, who are facing a large number of problems due to stiff neck-to-neck competition in every field of life. Growing use of advanced technology has further alienated them from the main stream of the society. This led him to initiate this book *Know Your Worth* with the young and enterprising writer Ms. Vibha Malhotra.

Vibha Malhotra

Vibha Malhotra is the founder of *Literature Studio* and editor-in-chief of the literary e-journal *Literature Studio Review*. In the past, she has worked as an editor with Dorling Kindersley (Penguin Random House) where she has edited beautiful coffee table books on subjects such as history, nature, fitness, lifestyle, and travel.

She is also a poet and a translator. Her work has been published in literary journals across the world such as *Wasafiri*, *Muse India*, *Tipton Poetry Journal*, *The Luxembourg Review*, *Red Fez*, and in dailies such as *The Times of India* and *Ceylon Today*. *Know Your Worth* is her first work as an author.

Vibha holds a Master of Arts in Creative Writing from Newcastle University, UK. She teaches creative writing to all age groups. By Profession, Vibha is a Lead Software Engineer at Adobe Systems.

KNOW YOUR WORTH

STOP THINKING, START DOING

N.K. SONDHI
VIBHA MALHOTRA

GENERAL PRESS

Published by
GENERAL PRESS
4228/1, Ansari Road, Daryaganj
New Delhi – 110002
Ph. : 011 – 23282971, 45795759
e-mail : generalpressindia@gmail.com

www.generalpress.in

First Edition : February 2017

ISBN : 9788180320231

Purchase our Books and eBooks online from:
Amazon.in, Snapdeal.com, Infibeam.com

Published by Azeem Ahmad Khan for General Press
Printed by Repro India Limited

Contents

Dedication   7

Introduction   9

1. Acknowledge Your Superpowers   13

2. Invest in Yourself   21

3. Take Charge   32

4. Set a Worthy Goal   37

5. Identify Your Worst Enemy   50

6. Turn Your Fear into an Opportunity   59

7. Avoid the Common Traps   70

8. Harvest the Power of Thoughts   103

9. Watch Your Attitude   119

10. Keep Your Communication Clear   140

11. Be Mindful   163

12. Surviving Bad Days   172

13. Nurture Your Ecosystem   194

14. Stay Successful   211

Dedication

This book is dedicated to all those readers who aspire to explore their own real worth in order to fight the odds of life and to achieve what they have set out to accomplish. This book is also dedicated to all those who we have looked up to for inspiration. Without you, this book wouldn't have been possible.

Disclaimer

This book contains views, experiences, observations, thoughts, vision, insights of several great achievers. In our lives, we have drawn inspirations from these thought leaders. These views, opinions, and incidents, have been cited in the book with the relevant credits. Apart from this, we have also included some long-forgotten folk tales of our childhood, that inspired us when we were young. These have been included so that our readers too can get inspired.

We have also included several contemporary anecdotes. The names, characters, places, and incidents are all imaginary. Any resemblance to real persons, living or dead, or actual events or localities, or organizations is purely coincidental.

Introduction

Are we our own worst enemies? This question can sound melo-dramatic, but in fact it is true for many of us, even if we do not realize it. Think about it. When was the last time you patted yourself on the back? Or treated yourself for your success? Our guess is that it has been a while. In fact many of you can't even remember when you last felt happy about something you did or the way you did it. Now try to remember the last time you felt like a failure or felt that you didn't handle a situation well. Many of you will be able to think of many such situations.

Now let us reverse this situation. Think about the people around you. Do you feel they are doing better than you? And if yes, are you able to find enough strength in yourself to feel happy for them? If your answer is "no", then the problem lies in how you perceive yourself. This may be slightly confusing right now, but the truth is that if you are happy with the way you are living your life and the things you are doing, you will find it easier to feel happy for others (even your rivals) for their achievements. However, the question is how do we reach such a state.

Our society at times is too protective of its young. Most of us, when we were growing up were never put in situations where we had to take decisions or assume positions of responsibility. We lead a sheltered life till we go to college and for many of us, this shelter continues even after we have graduated, started working, and have children of our own. Society tells us how we should lead our life. It dictates what is the measure of success and failure. It prescribes a strict code of conduct. In other words, it does everything it can to prevent us from thinking out-of-the-box.

Many of us grow older without actually growing up. We do not put enough energy and thought into learning precious lessons from life. We don't spend enough time exploring who we are and what can we do with our lives. We are afraid of dreaming big because we do not trust ourselves enough to achieve those dreams. We do not test and realize our strengths. To actually get to know ourselves, we have to depend on our own energies, strengths, confidence, and courage. These traits, unbeknownst to us, already exist in us. We all know that billions of people fail to live lives they dream of; the ones who fail to realize their ambitions and give up as soon as they encounter the first obstacle. On the other hand, we also know of several successful people who have started from the scratch and created great empires worth billions of dollars, but they are still fighting and continue to chase still bigger dreams.

Most of us wait for things to happen to us instead of making them happen. Then life puts us in a situation where we are suddenly forced to start growing up. We are forced to take charge and we realize that we can take charge of our lives too. In the context of this book, let us call such a moment the 'transformative moment'. And the purpose of this book is to precipitate that moment for you, to hasten it so that you can achieve things that you never thought yourself capable of.

Writing this book was a journey of self-discovery for us too. Hopefully we will be able to share some of those learnings too through this book. We hope that reading this book will be a fruitful journey for you too. With these hopes and prayers, let us together embark on this journey.

Acknowledge Your Superpowers

Knowing ourselves and knowing what we want to achieve in life is like the chicken and egg situation. Without knowing our strengths and weaknesses, it is difficult to figure out what is within our reach. And if we do not aim high, we can never challenge and overcome our weaknesses. So, understanding what we can and what we want to do in our lives is much more than a decision. It is a process. You need to give it time. You need to have patience.

The Story of the Young Man and Swami Vivekanand

Once upon a time, a young man was frustrated with his problems. For as long as he could remember, he had been

struggling hard and yet wasn't able to make both ends meet. He had grown up in a family of woodcutters, and had always longed for the luxuries enjoyed by people around him. However, the money he earned by selling wood couldn't buy him such a lifestyle.

He had tried working hard, but had failed. He had tried copying the ways of his more successful friends, but nothing had worked for him and his situation remained the same. His belief in himself and his abilities had plummeted. This is when he decided to consult Swami Vivekanand and seek his guidance.

Bowing to Swami Vivekanand, he asked humbly, "Swamiji, I have been struggling throughout my life, but I am still a poor woodcutter. I want to earn some money. Could you please guide me?" Swami Vivekanand looked at him and saw a young man with a robust physique.

"Why do you need money?" asked Swamiji.

"To live a joyful life," replied the woodcutter.

Swamiji then asked, "What are you willing to do to earn money?"

"I will do anything you ask me to do," replied the young man.

"Please be careful in what you commit," Swamiji cautioned him. "You cannot achieve anything without making sacrifices."

"I have thought this through. I will do anything for the sake of money," the young man repeated.

"Okay. Because you are so anxious for money, I will tell you a simple way to get lots of it, and that too instantly," Swamiji said with a smile.

Unsure whether Swamiji was serious, the young man replied, "If there is indeed such a way, I shall be very grateful if you can guide me. However, I am worried that Swamiji is joking. So far I haven't heard of any such way to earn instant money."

"Quick and big money comes with huge sacrifices. I am not joking. Indeed, I have a sound proposal for you. If you are ready to make sacrifices, you will certainly be successful in your mission."

"Swamiji, you are great. You are a very kind person. Whatever people told me about you is right," the young man gushed and bowed low to Swamiji. He waited anxiously for Swamiji to show him the way.

"There is a very rich man who lives close by. He is blind," said Swamiji. "His blindness can be cured if some-one donates him one eye. He is willing to pay a good amount to such a donor. If you donate one eye, you will not only be helping a handicapped person, but you will also get a lot of money in return. Moreover, you will still be left with one eye to enjoy a luxurious life. Can there be an easier way to earn so much money?"

The young man was horrified. He couldn't believe what Swamiji had just said. Giving one eye would mean forever losing the ability to see properly. The solution sounded terrible. But at the same time, the thought of earning a lot of money tempted him. "Moreover, Swamiji isn't asking me to donate both the eyes," thought the young man. "He is only asking me for one. Swamiji is right, with one eye I will still be able to enjoy my life."

Nevertheless, he decided to check what he was signing up for. He closed one of his eyes to see how life would be with just one functioning eye. Though Swamiji was right in front of him, the young man couldn't see his face. He turned his head left and then right but couldn't see the complete scene. He tried to count on his fingers but wasn't able to do so with one eye closed. Everything looked blurred and he was not able to judge distances. With this impaired vision, he would certainly not enjoy life. Moreover, he would not be able to get good employment and would be forced to start begging for livelihood, the very thought of which scared him. "No, I will not part with my eye. It is very precious to me," thought the woodcutter. He opened his eye and looked at Swamiji, and told him of his decision.

Swami Vivekanand agreed with his views, and gave him another option. He asked the young man to give him one of his hands and offered him Rs. Two Lacs in return. The young man expressed his unwillingness again. He refused to give his eye or hand for money.

Swamiji smiled and said, "You already are a rich man. You already possess everything that is most precious to human beings – intact body and good health. Recognize your own value. You are a human being and you can do whatever you wish to do, provided you first recognize your own worth."

We usually go about our lives like the young man in the above story. We have no idea of our powers.

Ex-President Late Shri A.P.J. Abdul Kalam once said:

"God, our creator, has stored in our minds and personalities, great potential strength and ability. We must tap and develop these powers."

Being ignorant of our power and energy, we make no efforts to fathom the depths of our real being. In fact, there is something amazing inside each of us and we must look for a way to nurture it and let it out.

However, we are largely unaware of these powers, simply because we only tend to believe in what is visible, audible, or apparent in any other way. However, these "superhuman" powers lie beneath the surface. Mostly they are dormant. But, at times they surface unexpectedly.

The first step to knowing ourselves is to have trust and belief in ourselves, but we often lose confidence at the first stumbling block. We start blaming our circumstances, unfavorable conditions, and start accepting the failures as our limitations. We blame ourselves for not being capable of handling situations, without really exploring different perspectives. We are therefore tempted to give up and try to be content with what we can obtain easily. How do we then harness these so-called "superpowers"?

Arun and the Dramatics Club

Consider the story of young Arun. His friends ran the Dramatics Club of their college. Arun had never really thought of himself as an actor. In fact, he believed that he had no talent in dramatics at all. He was an introvert and was afraid of speaking up in a group, so he tried to stay happy with just being the audience.

An inter-college street play competition was impending and the Dramatics Club was trying hard to come up with a powerful script for that. However, whatever they were coming up with sounded hollow and fake. Repeated discussions and attempts were bringing their morale down. Arun, as always, was carefully watching all this. At times, he felt that he knew exactly why one of their scripts wasn't working and what could be done to make it work. But because he thought that they knew their jobs better than he did, he couldn't muster the courage to offer suggestions.

However, after a while he couldn't bear to see his friends look so dejected. He thought there could be no harm in sharing what he felt. In a small, unsure voice, he said, "I feel…" No one heard him. So, he continued in a louder voice, "that your hero is too unbelievably noble. You should try to make him more like you and me, the common man. This will make your story more relatable." Now everyone was listening. They asked him to be more specific and initially were not completely receptive to his suggestions. But speaking up once had given him courage. He felt that he too could contribute. Therefore, he went on, "Your story is about the struggles of a common man, your hero needs to have faults and weaknesses like all of us do. Your story should depict how he overcomes internal and external challenges to emerge a victor." He pointed out at exactly what points the script could be tweaked so that the story became more relatable.

Gradually, everyone started seeing the merits in his suggestions and he was requested to assist the director of the play. Soon, the competition was over and their Dramatics Club had won. Arun couldn't believe the distance he had travelled over the last few days. From thinking that he had no talent in the area of dramatics, he had now successfully helped direct a play that had been loved by audience and critics alike.

From where did Arun suddenly get this talent? He, in fact, always had it in him. It was lying dormant, waiting for Arun to nurture it and to give it a chance to flourish.

The day we realize our true worth and the fact that we are capable of transcending the physical, emotional, and mental limitations we have imposed upon ourselves, we will certainly succeed where we had previously failed. So far, we chose weakness. When we choose power, we will positively become whatever we have chosen to be.

As an exercise, try to think of a really tough time in your life or a situation that you have now left behind. It could be losing someone close to you, or not landing a coveted job. It could be anything that made you feel that you can't go on or can't achieve something. Try to remember how you survived it, overcame it. What did you do to keep yourself sane during that time?

Did you know you could do it before you had actually gone ahead and done it? Do you now think you can handle the same situation again? Most probably, your answer is "yes" to this last question. The power that helped you overcome the situation was always there inside you. It helped you learn things about yourself that you did not know earlier. It helped you appreciate your human strengths. And it is still there waiting to be called to the surface, so that it can tell you more about yourself.

Now, take a moment and congratulate yourself for successfully overcoming the situation. Give yourself a pat on the back for the way you handled yourself during the challenge. It's okay to feel proud of yourself for this.

We do not do this enough. We do not appreciate ourselves enough. On the contrary, we are quick to find faults with everything we do. While it is okay to recognize your mistakes, and learn from them, it is equally important to acknowledge your strengths and successes. This will give you the confidence to carry on, and to achieve bigger goals. This will also help you hold your ground when you run into a tough situation again.

All the powers that you need to emerge a victor are already within you. You need to have faith in them. The creator has equipped you with all the weapons you need to fight any situation, and they will come to your rescue whenever there is a need, provided you believe in them.

Invest in Yourself

Now when you know that you have superpowers that are there within you and can be harvested whenever you need them, it is important to take time to really explore all your strengths and weaknesses. Only then can you be fully prepared to achieve your goals. But we are mostly clueless that understanding ourselves doesn't have to be a slow, tedious process, it can always be sped up.

All of us are born with inherent likes and dislikes. Even a fetus in the womb has its own taste preferences, resulting in the seemingly irrational food cravings that expecting mothers experience. These preferences, likes, and dislikes are clues to the things you will be good at. If a child enjoys painting more than singing, chances are that the child will be better at painting than he/she is at singing. You can think of these as clues that nature chose to expose to us so that we can carve a satisfying path for ourselves.

Most of us, even as adults, have whims, and mostly we choose to ignore them. Even as children, we are rarely able to indulge in every whim. There are always limitations – in terms of time, finances, facilities etc. – to keep us from fully exploring what we are capable of. But these are not the only factors that stop us. The biggest factor, in fact, is our own inhibitions, especially once we are grown-ups. We are afraid of new experiences, afraid of disappointment, afraid of failure, afraid of making fools of ourselves. And this fear keeps us from taking advantage of opportunities to gather new experiences. Let us try to understand this with the example of a young girl called Shikha.

Shikha and the Ideation Competition

Shikha was an editor at a publishing house. She was very good at her job and apart from being an excellent editor, she also often proposed new book ideas to the publishing house.

The publishing house announced a competition in which teams would work together and come up with new book ideas that they would then present to a jury comprising of senior publishers from all over the world. The selected idea would then be converted into a book that would be sold all over the world.

Shikha had never ever participated in a competition, let alone won it. She wasn't at all confident of her abilities to work in a team. And the fact that the competition was

*about new book ideas was making her restless. By propos-
ing new book ideas in the past, she had earned a reputation in that area. Her colleagues and even her boss thought
of her as a creative thinker. Shikha was worried that if she
participated in this competition and lost it, her reputation
as a creative thinker would be tarnished too. Can you
guess why she was so full of doubts? It was because she had
always attributed her past achievements to good luck, and
had never given herself any credit for the book ideas she
had come up with. Thus, she was afraid of being exposed
as someone who really did not possess any great talent.*

*She was still in this state of dilemma when she discov-
ered that her manager had already nominated Shikha's
name for the competition. Now she had no choice, so she
decided to go with the flow. With each passing day, her
desperation to win the contest increased, and by the time
the date of the competition arrived, she found herself
unable to sleep. She knew that she would do anything
to win this competition. For the first time in her life she
was this passionate about something. She wanted to give
it her all.*

*On the day of the competition, she was put in a team
and the team started with discussing the various ideas
that all members had. Shikha had a great idea, but when
she saw more merit in the idea proposed by another team
member, she voted for it to be taken up for further prepa-
ration and the final presentation. She was almost feverish
with excitement. And when her team members were of
the opinion that they should give their best and not really
care if they win or lose, Shikha was single-minded about*

her goal of winning the competition. Her focus proved to be contagious and soon all her team-members too were bubbling with enthusiasm. Guided by their single goal, the group of strangers really became a team and the initial idea evolved to become something they all believed in. Though the team leader was someone else, everyone could see that Shikha was the driving force for the team. When it was time to present their idea, the team leader proposed that Shikha should do it. And the presentation left the judges mesmerized. When their team emerged the winner, no one was surprised. Their idea and their presentation of it were deemed to be the best.

Once she was out of the competition frenzy, Shikha herself was surprised. She couldn't understand what had come over her during the competition. But she was glad to discover this other Shikha. She had gone into the competition based on her creative thinking, but her team had emerged a winner because of her team spirit and leadership skills. Shikha was surprised to discover these two new skills in herself. She had never thought herself capable of what she had achieved.

Most of us are like Shikha – capable, but afraid of failure and public ridicule. And this is why we do not take chances in life. We like to play safe. But one can never really truly understand oneself by remaining in a shell. Unless you experience new things, you can never experience a new you. Unless you take risks, you can never transcend your normal, day-to-day existence.

But, what gives us the capacity to take risks? Our confidence on our strengths and abilities. And from where do we get this confidence? Unfortunately, it isn't a commodity and you cannot buy it from a shop. Money can't buy you confidence. You need to work hard to develop it. You need to test yourself, which is again done by putting yourself in situations that you feel are beyond your reach. So, this is once again a chicken-and-egg situation. But after you have been through some such cycles and are confident of the situations you can handle, you are in a better position to fix your goals.

However, it is easier said than done. Unfortunately, life is not a fairy tale and this means that we will not succeed every time we take up a challenge. There will also be times when we fail. This is inevitable. We will invariably have to face problems, and this may shake our confidence. Dealing with failures is not easy. It is like a double-edged sword. If you take failures too seriously, they may end up crushing you. On the other hand, if you take them too lightly, you will not learn any lessons from them, which means that the risk that you took would go to waste. So, you need to recognize failures for what they are – failures. Nothing more, nothing less. If you fail in a challenge, it does not mean that you yourself are a failure. This is the most common mistake we commit. Failing a challenge means that you failed that challenge. You need to analyze the situation, see what you could have done better, and move on to the next challenge where you can test your learnings.

This act of never giving up, will give you confidence and this confidence helps us realize our capabilities. And this, in turn, shows in our personality. We hold our head high. We walk with determination. We talk with conviction, and we are normally in a good mood. Confidence also gives us perseverance – the ability to keep going after a failure. If you haven't invested in yourself, you are more likely to give up after a failure or two.

Confidence helps us stay on our path and not go astray. Many hurdles and problems may block our way and discourage us, but if we have confidence, we will not let these hurdles stop us. Instead we will search for an alternate path to our goal.

The Little Bird and the Branch

Once a little bird landed on a branch high up a tall tree. The jungle below was full of dangerous predators but at this height, they posed no danger to the little bird. Feeling safe and protected, the little bird rested, enjoying the beautiful view around, and feeling completely at peace. Just as the bird became used to the branch, a strong wind started blowing, shaking the entire tree. The tree swayed with such intensity that it appeared the branch would break and fall down.

To other animals, this could be a matter of great worry, but the little bird was not worried. Do you know why? Because the little bird knew its own powers and strengths. Even if the branch was to fall down, the bird knew that it had wings and the ability to fly. And the bird was also aware that if this branch was to fall, there are many other branches that could be used instead. Therefore, the bird, though tiny in size, sat on the branch, braving the high wind. The animals below, all of them much stronger than the bird, were filled with much admiration

for this courageous little creature who was braving diffi-
cult circumstances.

The story of this small bird tells us a lot about our own self-confidence and courage. If one road is blocked there are others we can follow. And if there are no new roads, there's always the earth on which we can make a new road.

When we start believing in our own power and energy we will find there are many branches and trees available for our safety and security. But such security and safety measures do not always last. Long-lasting and permanent measures rest within ourselves in the form of self-esteem and belief in our own capabilities. If we believe that we can overcome any setback, we will fear nothing. And when we are secure in this knowledge, we are not afraid to be ourselves in any situation.

As an exercise, let us analyze our own day-to-day actions. We are mere humans with no ability to look into the future. Despite this, we plan big things for tomorrow. We save for retirement, we invest for our kids, and we sacrifice on luxury today so that we can have a comfortable life when we are older. From where do we get this confidence? The answer is simple. We have learnt from the experiences of our parents, of people around us. But there is also another aspect to this. We are programmed by default to think positive. And this is one of our strongest powers. But we will come to this later. For now, let us talk a little more about confidence.

Preran and the Uncashed Cheque

Preran, a very successful businessman, fell ill and remained bed-ridden for a few months. In his absence, his business suffered and ran into losses. After recovering from the illness, Preran faced acute difficulties as he was under huge debt and could see no way out of the situation. He was on the verge of bankruptcy. To top it all, his creditors started mounting pressure and the suppliers were demanding payment. Weakened by illness, he found managing his affairs extremely difficult. Unable to find any financial help, Preran felt overwhelmed by stress.

It was in this condition of mental turmoil that he was walking down the street towards his office, when he collided with a well-dressed gentleman wearing a business suit and a tie. Preran fell down because of the collision, and the gentleman helped him back on his feet. Preran rendered a half-hearted apology and started to walk away.

But the gentleman called him back and asked him what was wrong. Preran, moved by the concern in the gentleman's voice, poured his heart out to this complete stranger. The gentleman listened patiently and offered Preran money immediately on the condition that he would return the same to him within one year. Preran could not believe his luck. He looked at the gentleman, trying to figure out whether he was joking. But he could see the gentleman was very serious. Preran thanked God for sending an angel to help him in these tough times.

In the meantime, the gentleman asked for his name and issued him a check of a huge amount and left without speaking another word. Preran looked at the check; the amount written on it was enough to solve all his financial problems immediately. He wondered whether it was God who had met him in the guise of the gentleman and helped him. Preran wanted to thank the gentleman, but he had already left. Preran decided to return the money with interest, but realized that in his state of shock, he had forgotten to ask the gentleman his name, address, or phone number.

Now that he had the check, Preran's confidence returned. He was filled with a conviction that things would work out no matter what. The possibility of having instant cash in hand rejuvenated his optimism and he plunged himself into his work with all his heart. He kept on putting off converting the check simply because he was in the possession of the check. He acquired the required strength to work out a way to save his business. He was an expert businessman; he negotiated better deals and got the terms of payments rescheduled. He even managed to close several big deals. Within a few months he was out of the debt and started making profit. All this while, the check remained in his possession, uncashed.

Very soon he realized that he did not need the check after all and wished he could return it to the gentleman. He started searching for the gentleman, but despite an expansive and intensive search, he could not find him. Instead of keeping the check unutilized, he decided to encash it and keep the money in a Fixed Deposit account so that it could earn some interest. Whenever he would meet the gentleman next he could then return him his money with interest. But the check in question bounced and was returned with the following remarks:

"Insufficient balance. The account belongs to a person of unsound mind."

Preran was surprised to know this. All this long he had been dealing, buying and selling, executing orders convinced that he had a huge amount of money available to him. This money turned out to be imaginary, but it had still turned his life around. He realized that in the end it was only his confidence and self-belief that had caused this. He was an able businessman and always had it in him to rebuild his empire.

Like Preran, most of us are also held back because of self-doubt. Our skills and strengths always remain with us; we only need to have faith. If you are good at painting, no calamity can take it away from you. Circumstances may make you feel that you will never be able to paint again, but that is simply not true. The talent is there, you just need to believe in it.

In order to discover your strengths and talents, you need to put yourself in situations where you will be forced to go beyond your normal day-to-day existence, do things that you don't usually do in your daily life. Once you have discovered your strengths, you need to practice relentlessly in order to polish them and become a master. There is no easy way around this. Ask any artist. You need years of *riyaaz* to become a maestro. It is the same with any other skill and strength. To become an able leader, you need to work hard and rise through the ranks. To become a good engineer, you need to work on challenging projects and learn, and learn, and learn. Don't wait for life to give you these opportunities, rise up and grab them. This is the only way to fast-track your growth.

If your strengths are your armor, your weaknesses are like a crack in it. Everyone has weaknesses. They are there inside you, waiting to surface unexpectedly and create havoc in your life. While Preran suffered because of illness, which is an external factor, most of us fail because of internal factors. Consider this example, and replace the skill "writing" with any other skill of your liking. Imagine you are a great writer, capable of weaving magic with your words. But if you lack the discipline to sit down and work dedicatedly on a project (for example, a book), you will find it very difficult to ever make something out of your abilities. Your weakness will be ready to drag you down at the first instance. So while you test yourself for your strengths by putting yourself through challenges, also use these opportunities to test yourself for your weaknesses. To emerge a victor, you not only need to master your skills, you also need to overcome weaknesses. While in some cases, you may need to take up special trainings to overcome a weakness (for example, public speaking), in most cases, simply being aware of them is enough. This will help you keep a watch on yourself, and to wake up at the first sign of trouble. If you know your enemies, you can always be better prepared to handle them. This is the case with your weaknesses too. If you are aware of them, they cannot take you by surprise.

Therefore, take some time. Realize your strengths and acknowledge your weaknesses. This is all that it takes in most cases to help you achieve your dreams.

Take Charge

Now you know that you have superpowers, and also that by putting yourself through challenges you will understand yourself better. The next step is to start taking charge of your life. It is time to decide what you want to do. Most of us never think of setting any goals. We prefer to go with the flow.

But don't most people manage perfectly well without setting goals? They do. But do they achieve their full potential? Do they reach where they could have reached with a little planning? Our guess is no, they don't. And apart from this, there are other reasons why it is beneficial to set goals. Let us talk about them.

GOALS HELP IN PLANNING

If you want to be productive in life, you need to think of things in terms of projects. And as in any project, you need to plan and execute in a way that you achieve the predetermined result within the decided timeframe. A goal helps you do just that. It helps you in planning your moves in a way so that you can achieve what you want to achieve in time.

GOALS PREVENT DISTRACTION

It is easy to get distracted when you do not have a deadline looming or when you do not have a definite plan with timelines. Having a goal helps you stay focused.

Bill Copeland, American poet, writer, and historian, said:

"The trouble with not having a goal is that you can spend your life running up and down the field and never score."

Isn't this true? Consider the simple example of a To-do list. Many of us maintain a list of tasks that we need to complete within the day. This is like setting a mini-goal for ourselves. It helps us plan, prioritize, and efficiently execute the tasks. It also helps us make an informed decision in case we feel that we would need to defer some tasks from the list. It also prevents us from spending time on unproductive activities. Setting a goal is exactly like this. If you have your goal in sight, you can plan backwards and stay focused.

GOALS GIVE US A PURPOSE

When you have your goal in sight, and you know what you have to do and how you have to do it, your entire demeanor changes. You go about your life confidently, and are almost never confused or undecided. It gives you a sense of pride and that shows in how you carry yourself. It gives you a good reason to wake up in the morning. It keeps you away from idle wanderings of the mind that can be very dangerous in the long run. Having a goal is not only good for your professional growth, it is important for your spiritual and mental growth too.

The Obese Man and his Daughter

An obese man was advised by his doctor to exercise and lose weight. But he turned a deaf ear to the suggestions. He had a little daughter. One day, the daughter came home crying from the school. When asked the reason, she told that her best friend's name had been struck off from the rolls of the school. Apparently, her father had died and her school fees hadn't been paid for many months.

This set the obese man thinking. What would happen if he were to die one day? Would his daughter too be shunted out of the school? The thought itself was too terrible for him. He knew he was at constant risk of various diseases because of his weight. He decided to do something immediately. From then on, he set a weight goal for himself and started exercising as advised by the doctor. He now had a purpose, and he went about doing everything for it.

Soon he had started losing weight. Not only was he feeling more secure, he was also feeling more confident and cheerful. By giving him a purpose, the goal had changed him as a person.

GOALS MAKE US ACCOUNTABLE

Accountability means an obligation or willingness to accept responsibility and to be responsible for one's actions and their results. When we set a goal for ourselves we make ourselves accountable to finish the task in the given time. We can no longer give excuses or work as per our convenience. We are pushed to chalk out a course of action and adhere to it. Whether or not we achieve our goal becomes our responsibility.

GOALS ARE A SOURCE OF ENTHUSIASM

We have already discussed how goals give us a sense of purpose. When we set a goal for ourselves, we automatically start imagining our lives after we have achieved the goal or the impact our achieving the goal can have on others. Consider the example of an NGO. When an NGO starts a fund-raising drive, they already have an amount in mind and the impact that money is going to have on their cause. This thought itself is enough to make them feel excited about the drive. Sense of purpose, along with accountability and excitement, are enough to transform you as a person. This is enough to fill your life with positive energy.

GOALS KEEP US GOING

Fixing a goal means that we endeavor to reach its end within a finite time by setting deadlines. Once the task starts we tend to see our progress on day-to-day basis. We are constantly aware of what we have done so far and how long it would take to complete the rest. This constant planning keeps us going.

Indeed, without goals we end up wasting a lot of time in fruitless activities. It is more challenging to keep ourselves motivated and in a positive frame of mind. Without goals, it is impossible to measure our progress as a human being, as a student, as a professional, or as anyone in any field or stage of life. Without goals, it is impossible to stay focused. Without goals, we are all drifters. With goals, we are in charge.

Set a Worthy Goal

You know you have superpowers. You also know that you are equipped with all the weapons to enable you to fight your battles. You are aware that you need to put yourself through challenging situations to get to know yourself well. And you also know that you need to set goals for yourself in order to make your life as productive as it can be.

Setting a goal is as much a science as it is an art. Setting a relevant goal can take you closer to what you ultimately want to achieve, whereas setting an irrelevant goal can distract you from your path and end up wasting your time. By this, we do not mean that you should not indulge in activities that do not align with your goal. By all means you should. It is important to indulge in things you enjoy, though they may not always be means to an end. Hanging out with friends, playing games, travelling, watching movies – everything counts. But we will go there later. This chapter is about how you can make the most of your goals.

If you truly want to live to the fullest, you need to think your goals through. There are two ways to approach this. The first is to be aware of your larger goal – what you want to achieve in the long run – and then have short-term goals to help you achieve the long-term goal. This is the ideal way to plan your life. However, we know that in life things are often far from ideal. Forget about having a long-term vision; very often we do not know what we want to do next. In this case, how do we go about planning and living our life to the fullest. If you find yourself in this situation, the best approach is to start with short-term goals about things that excite you. This will not only expose you to multiple ideas, it will also help you get into the habit of setting goals and achieving them. In time, you may be able to figure out your long-term goal, and then you will be better prepared to achieve it.

If you are planning to start setting goals for yourself now, it is important for you to know what we are going to talk about next. What is it that makes some people more successful at achieving their goals? Of course, it depends upon everyone's individual personality (which we will discuss in later chapters), but it also depends upon the kind of goals they set. Following are some things that you should keep in mind when setting a goal:

1. Dreams and Goals are Different and Require Different Treatments

The mistake we make most often is that we confuse our dreams with our goals. And this is understandable. A dream can be turned into a long-term goal. But most often, it is so long term that we lose our momentum midway. Consider the example of a software engineer who wants to own a villa in the hills with lawns and fields around it. He/she wants to get into farming too and adopt farm animals. In short, he not only wants to buy land and construct a villa, he also wants to become an expert in rural lifestyle. This is clearly a really long-term goal. It is, in fact, a dream. Let us now try to convert this dream into goals.

The first step the Software engineer needs to take is to test himself. Is this really what he wants to do, or is this only an escapist's fantasy – a way to deal with the monotony and stress of his everyday life? Once he has done that and he is sure that he wants to do it, the next step is to identify what it would take to make this dream a reality. He would need an estimate of how much investment he would need to make to purchase the land, to build his house, to buy animals. He will need to know what will be the impact on his income and plan resources so that he has enough money saved up to back him up when he is setting up his farm (assuming he leaves his job to do this). He also needs to prepare himself for the drastic cut in income. Apart from this, over the time he also needs to prepare himself to let go of other conveniences available in an urban setting – high-speed internet connection, readily available medical facilities, regular interactions with friends etc. Once he is done doing all the homework, he will need to do the actual legwork. Which would mean searching for a land, buying it, getting the house built, buying animals, hiring the required helps etc. Getting used to the hectic daily routine – because managing a farm is far more difficult than it appears from a distance. So you can see that each of these tasks in itself can be a long-term goal. While keeping your eyes on your dream or your final destination, you should plan for your long-term goals.

Your journey towards your dream is a path full of self-discovery. A dream can also be your goal. The very thought of achieving your dream makes your stomach flutter with excitement. On the other hand, goals are your plans, procedures, actions and attempts to get to your dream. In other words, goals are your dreams with feet. Or as Swami Vivekanand has said:

> *"Take up one idea. Make that one idea your life – think of it, dream of it and live on that idea. Let the brain, muscles, nerves, every part of your body, be full of that idea, and just leave every other idea alone. This is the way to success."*

That one idea is your dream, your very purpose in life.

2. Be Realistic While Setting Goals

If, in the above example, the Software Engineer sets a goal that "I will have my farm up and running within the next six months", what would you think of the goal? Do you think the goal is achievable? And even if by some means the software engineer does manage to procure a farm and get things rolling, do you think he would have done the required homework that would help him take the best decision? Do you think he would have thought everything through? Do you think by being in hurry, the engineer would have done justice to his dream?

When you are setting your goal, make sure you select something that is humanly possible. If you haven't run in the last 10 years, you cannot expect yourself to run a marathon within a week. Even if you do manage somehow, it isn't good for your health. So this is definitely not a good goal to set. Be practical and don't be in a hurry. Set a goal that is achievable within the timeframe. And give yourself enough time to achieve it.

Let us go back to the example of the Software Engineer who is a wannabe farmer. Imagine if that Software Engineer was to buy a farm in a hurry, buy animals in a hurry, sow seeds without giving it much thought, without even waiting for the right season. What would happen in that case? Will the farm flourish? Will the Software Engineer actually be able to reap the rewards of setting a goal and achieving it? On the contrary, his plans will most probably fall flat if he goes about them without patience. He will end up feeling demotivated and is likely to give up on his dream. You can avoid this situation by planning well, by having realistic expectations from yourself, and by allowing yourself enough time to achieve your goal in a way such that it doesn't slip through your fingers like sand.

3. Set a Goal that is Measurable

Consider someone on a fitness drive. Suppose this person sets himself the following goal – *"I will become fit."* What is the first thing you notice about this goal? It is pretty vague. The goal setter does not talk about exactly what being "fit" means here. Does it mean that this person wants to lose weight? Does it mean that he wants to control his blood pressure, or diabetes, or cholesterol? Does it mean that he wants to acquire 6-pack abs? Or does he want to increase his stamina? Therefore, there is no way to verify whether this goal has been met. This person will need to make his goal more specific. So probably a goal that says *"I will lose 10 kg"* is better.

Now we come to the second aspect of it. Have you ever tried to set yourself a goal without a definite timeline? What happens if you do try this? Most humans are wired in such a way that they cannot focus on a goal until and unless there is a deadline looming, or unless you at least have some idea about how much time has passed and how much still remains. In fact, timelines do much more than just put pressure on you. They help in measuring your progress. And this can be a good motivating factor too. So, it is important to have a definite timeline. Therefore, the following goal will be much better – *"I will lose 10 kg in six months starting today."* Better still, specify a date. This date will get imprinted in your mind and it will be easier to gauge progress.

Once you have set a measurable goal, you know exactly what you want to achieve and by when you will achieve it.

Once your final goal is shaped up, you can start backward planning and set mini goals to ensure you reach your final goal. The rule for these mini goals is also the same. They, too, should be measurable.

4. Make Sure the Goal is Worth it

Let us take the example of a professional situation to explain this point. Consider that you are eyeing a promotion and you feel that developing a new tool to streamline a process that your team follows would do it for you. You have thought of a tool, and you set a goal for yourself that you will complete developing the tool within 3 months. You start planning backwards. You set your mini-goals. You work hard to achieve them. You develop and test and develop and test. You get your tool reviewed by your peers. You do trial runs. In short, you put in a lot of effort and are able to achieve your goal. Your tool is up and running! Yay! Next, you show it to your manager. He really appreciates your work on the tool. And then comes the appraisal time. You are sure you will be promoted. But it turns out you aren't. What went wrong?

Your boss tells you that though you showed initiative and you were a good performer, you aren't amongst the top. You vehemently say that you created the tool. The boss agreed that it was a good thought and that may help the organization in the long run, but there are other people in your organization who have done things that are already showing results and have managed to catch senior management's attention. It was easier for your boss to convince the senior management to promote those colleagues. You are heartbroken. After all, you worked so hard. So where did you go wrong? You did not do your homework. You did not share your aspirations and plans with your boss. You did not try to find out the organization's priorities. You did not try to see where your peers stand and what are they doing to fulfill their aspirations. With this in mind, was the end result really worth it? Did achieving your goal take you closer to your dream of getting a promotion? No. This goal was definitely not worth all the effort you put in to achieve it.

This is one situation that you may come across after years of working in the corporate sector. In fact, some people never learn it. However, the earlier you learn this lesson, the better it is for your professional growth.

5. Make Sure that the Goal Actually Excites You

Our society is such that we are used to doing things that do not really excite us without ever questioning them. For example, taking up science in school instead of arts or commerce. Studying to become an engineer or a doctor. Doing a management degree. Marrying. Having Children. And so on. And once we have been through this cycle, we make all efforts to ensure that our children, too, conform to the tried and tested route, that they fall in line. We only choose an alternate route when we are left with no option. The fact that we can choose to not do any of these things simply because we do not want to do them never really occurs to us. We aren't used to making choices based on what we actually want to do. This way of being is so deeply etched in our personalities that we never question it. And this is why we often make the same mistake while setting our goals too.

Consider the example of two sisters – the elder one has been very clear right from the very beginning that she wants to be a doctor. All her efforts are, therefore, directed towards this. She chooses science in her secondary school. She takes coaching for medical entrance. She appears for her exams and very soon is a qualified doctor. However, the younger one has grown up in the shadow of her elder sister. She has seen her sister being appreciated for what she is doing. So she feels that probably she should aspire for the same. She, too, should become a doctor. So, she too chooses science in her secondary school, though she loves to write and paint. She takes up coaching as her sister had done and appears for the entrance exam. However, she does not clear them and gives up after the first attempt. Why do you think this happened?

It is simply because the younger sister was never as passionate about becoming a doctor as the elder one. She loved writing and the thought of studying huge medical text books for half-a-decade simply did not excite her. So she ended up wasting her time and her parents' money and energy.

This girl was probably too young to understand what was at stake, but many of us do not understand this even when we are older. We keep doing things that do not interest us because we think that is the "right" thing to do. Aspiring to become a manager in a corporate firm, even though you are not really interested in managing people is another such example. Many corporate offices now offer a parallel growth path along with the managerial one. But very few of us are brave enough to take that. The society expects you to become a manager after certain number of years in service and unless you fulfill this expectation, you will be branded as an under-achiever. So you go on and do what the generation before you had done, despite the fact that your heart is elsewhere. This is the greatest disservice you can do to yourself.

Career is a huge deal. We do not even feel confident of exercising our choices when the goals are much smaller. There is a competition that everyone is participating in, you put your name in it. There's a party that everyone's going for, you go for it too. There's this new technology that everyone is learning, you go and learn it too. You do this without ever being aware that you can choose otherwise. You can choose not to participate in that competition, not to go for that party, and not to learn that new technology. Instead, you can invest your efforts in doing something you really want to do. And once you do that, you will be surprised at the passion with which you step towards your goal. You will no longer feel inclined to give up midway. This probably is the most important learning from this point. And it is valid in almost all other aspects of our lives too.

6. Make Sure that You are Interested in the Journey too

Let us again go back to the example of the two sisters to understand this point. Suppose the younger one is really interested in becoming the Chief Minister of Delhi. The amount of power the Chief Minister enjoys really excites her. She sees how much respect the Chief Minister receives from people around us. She loves the thought that the Chief Minister can effectively transform a city. So she asks her parents whether this is a good idea. Her parents do not want to discourage her, but since they have already witnessed the doctor fiasco, they want to make sure their daughter really knows her mind this time.

So they decide to take their daughter on a virtual tour about what it takes to be a politician. They show her what a party-worker is required to do, since that is where she will need to start. They show her how the student unions work. They make her listen to the speeches of the leaders of the student wings of major political parties. They make her read the news clips about how contrary the real-life actions of these leaders can be to their words. In short they show her the kind of life she will have to lead for a long, long time if she wants to ultimately become a political leader. If after knowing all this, she is still ready to withstand the challenges, she will most probably be able to survive the journey. However, if the journey scares her or does not excite her, then she better choose something else.

Especially in the case of a long-term goal, make sure you choose a goal that you would want to achieve even if the journey is tough. In short, the journey itself should also excite you.

7. Make Sure You set a Goal that is in Your Control

At times we end up setting goals for ourselves, the end result of which is not exactly in our control. Consider, for example, the corporate employee who is eyeing a promotion. Do you think that the employee can really set the following goal – *"I will be promoted by the end of this year?"* Not really. Because whether or not he gets promoted is not really in his control. He can work hard, he can communicate his aspirations, he can do everything in his power to make himself eligible for a promotion. But in the end whether he gets promoted or not depends upon the decision of the senior management. So there is no point setting such a goal. A goal, the end result of which is not entirely in your control, is in fact a dream. If you find yourself in such a situation, step back and evaluate. Ask yourself, what is the last goal that you will need to achieve in order to make this dream probable? Set that as your goal. That is the maximum you can do. Don't worry about what happens after this. That is up to those who control it.

8. Make Sure You Make Your Goal Real

Once you are done setting your goal, write it down somewhere so that it actually exists in a physical form. Make sure that it is always in sight. Also inform someone you trust about this. It can be a friend, a sibling, or anyone who can hold you accountable for it. Try to select someone you respect immensely and do not want to disappoint. Prepare your schedule to achieve this goal and also give a copy of the schedule to this person. Make this person a stakeholder. Ask him/her to act as your timekeeper for this. Ask this person to nag you endlessly if you are missing or about to miss your deadlines. Ask this person to follow up with you on your deadlines proactively.

Introducing another person in this scenario not only makes you want to achieve your goal more desperately, it also keeps you on your toes. Suddenly the perceived risk associated with the failure to achieve your goal increases. You will not only be answerable to yourself if you do not put in enough efforts, you will also have to answer another person. Another person will also be aware of your failure in case you do not give this goal your best. We have been raised on the mantra, "What will people say?" so this will probably prove to be the most effective technique to keep you on track.

Once you have written your goal down and confided in one person you trust, you have concretized your goal and made it more real. There are higher chances of you achieving this goal now.

Once you have set your goal, the next step is to obviously start following your plan and achieving your mini-goals. For this, you need to hone some special abilities. We will talk about these in the next few chapters.

Identify Your Worst Enemy

You now know that you have superpowers, you understand yourself a little better, and you have also analyzed and set a worthy goal for yourself. What do you do next? Of course you go about achieving those goals. But before we talk about how to do this, it is important to understand the biggest hurdle we are likely to encounter during our journey. Can you take a guess at it? Let us give you a hint. It is not a physical entity. It is not even an external entity. It is internal to you. It is a trait that is common to all human beings, in fact, all living beings. It is nothing but *fear*.

The one single entity that most often keeps us from achieving our full potential is fear – more specifically, fear of failure. No matter how hard we work, no matter how well we handle our jobs, no matter how good we are at it, somewhere deep inside, we have that slight doubt that we are not good enough. This doubt manifests into a fear of failure whenever we take up a challenge. We worry that we will fail to achieve our goal and our friends, family, colleagues, acquaintances, even random strangers will see us for the *fake people* we are. We will, forever, lose their respect for us. We will become someone who cannot be trusted with positions of responsibility.

This fear of failure then leads us to do many things, such as avoid taking up tasks that are challenging, or try to think up excuses we will make if we fail to achieve this task, even before we have actually started with the task itself. Needless to say, this negative mindset doesn't help us in achieving our full potential.

The fear of failure is such an ancient hurdle that it even finds mention in the *Bhagavad Gita*. Here is a translation (by Ramananda Prasad) of one such quotation:

> *"You have control over doing your respective duty, but no control or claim over the result. Fear of failure, from being emotionally attached to the fruit of work, is the greatest impediment to success because it robs efficiency by constantly disturbing the equanimity of mind."*

Fear stops us from becoming our best. It quickly becomes our biggest weakness and acts as an obstacle to building up on our strengths. Our fear can overshadow our confidence in our strengths. It is our fear of failure that can stop us from giving our best to the task at hand.

Let us understand this further with the help of a popular story. This is one of the *Panchatantra* tales and many of you would probably have already read it.

The Sage and the Mouse

Once upon a time, deep inside a dense forest lived a sage. Every morning, creatures from all over the forest would gather around him to listen to his spiritual preaching. They would listen intently as the sage meditated and told them about the good things in life. These animals would collect whatever food they could find and offer it to the sage. The sage would keep some for himself and distribute the rest amongst all the creatures who were his disciples.

In the same forest, there also lived a little mouse. He was also one of the sage's disciples and visited the great man every day. One day, when this mouse was roaming around in the woods looking for berries he could bring to the sage, he was attacked by a big cat, who had been keeping a watch on him for some time from behind the wild bushes.

The mouse somehow managed to escape but was scared. He ran straight to the sage. The sage took note of the sorry state the mouse was in and asked what was wrong. The mouse lay prostrate before the sage and told him about the cat and the vicious attack. In the meanwhile, the cat who had been following the mouse also ended up in the sage's ashram and politely requested the sage to let him eat the mouse as it was his prey.

Now the sage was in a dilemma. He could only help one of them. He considered the situation for a moment and then taking pity on the weaker party transformed the mouse into a bigger cat. Seeing this huge cat, the smaller cat ran away.

The mouse, who was now a cat, was free of fear. He began to freely roam about in the forest. He challenged other cats and killed many of them in fights. He was full of revenge for the terror the cats had wrecked on his fellow mice.

The mouse was just getting comfortable in his skin as a cat, when one day a dog attacked him. This was an unprecedented situation for the mouse. As a mouse, he had never really considered animals bigger than cats as they most often ignored him. Now the realization dawned upon him that there were animals more ferocious than a cat that could easily kill him. Once again he somehow dodged the dog and ended up at the sage's feet. The dog too gave a chase and soon both of them stood in front of the sage.

The sage once again took pity on the mouse and turned him into a great, big dog. Seeing a dog bigger than himself close by, the other dog ran away.

The mouse, who was now a dog, once again started roaming around the jungle without fear. He would howl in the night and growl during the day. He would bare his fangs to any creature who happened to cross its path. But this too proved to be short-lived.

One day on his way to the river, he came across a ferocious tiger. The tiger pounced upon the dog and almost managed to kill him. The dog somehow managed to wriggle free and once again ran to his savior – the sage. The tiger gave a chase and the dog and the tiger soon stood side-by-side in front of the sage.

The sage considered the situation and seeing no harm in his action, he transformed the dog into a huge, ferocious tiger. The other tiger vanished into the jungle at the sight of the bigger tiger.

Now, the tiger, who was once a dog who was once a cat who was once a mouse, forgot all humility. He roamed around the jungle and ruled over the other animals as their king. He killed innocent beings for no fault of theirs, for no purpose at all. He killed for fun, when he was bored, when he was angry. Other animals all began to fear this ferocious tiger who had learnt to kill even when he wasn't hungry.

However, the tiger himself wasn't completely at ease. This was because he still had one fear, one that did not let him sleep. He was painfully aware of the fact that it was because of the sage that he was now a tiger. And he knew that the sage could transform him back into a mouse whenever her wanted. Ultimately, he decided that he had had enough, and the only way he could be free was when the sage was dead. He went roaring to the sage's ashram. The sage sensed what was going on in the tiger's mind. He had so far been patient with this mouse in a tiger's form but now he became really angry. In an instant, he transformed the tiger into the mouse that he originally was.

The mouse's worst fear had come true, and now he realized his mistake. However, it was too late. Even though he apologized profusely to the sage, the sage had lost faith in the mouse's ability to handle power. He simply shooed him away with a stick.

This little story teaches us several lessons. The mouse is never free of fear, whether he is a mouse, a cat, a dog, or even when he is a tiger. It is the same case with us. If we overpower one fear, another is always ready to grip us. As human beings, we can never be free of fear. Many a times we create our own fears. Most of us live our lives under one or more fears. Fear of failure, fear of losing our loved ones, fear of our boss, parents, or elders, fear of being unsuccessful, fear of death. We are not able to do what we are capable of doing only because of this deadly disease called *fear*. If we try to run away from fear, it chases us even more relentlessly and may succeed in overpowering us – like in the case of the mouse who invited its own downfall by deciding to kill the sage.

It's our instinct of fear that really keeps us chained to our limiting beliefs and insecurities and holds us back from using our inherent superpowers. Fear is simply because we are not just living, we are living with our mind. We are rushing ahead, imagining the worst possible outcomes of our actions. Our main fear is always what is going to happen next. We think of everything that can go wrong. We think about the situations that do not exist. If the situation does not exist at present, it means our fear is just in our imagination and not for real.

Some specialists categorize fear as an unpleasant emotion or thought. Indeed it is nothing more than that. Even though our fear becomes real to us in our imagination, it is really nothing but a feeling. And this feeling becomes one of the greatest impediments to our growth. The element of fear adversely influences our actions and decisions. Our fear becomes the biggest cause of us undermining our abilities and, in turn, losing our confidence.

As per Swami Vivekanand:

"Be not afraid of anything. You will do marvellous work. The moment you fear, you are nobody. It is fear that is the great cause of misery in the world. It is fear that is the greatest of all superstitions. It is fear that is the cause of our woes, and it is fearlessness that brings heaven even in a moment."

There are situations in life that scare us and make us want to escape, but if we do, they will chase us down and take over our life. In such situations, our thoughts become dominated by the things that we are afraid of and our actions become timid and cautious, not allowing us to reach our full potential.

Think of this very common situation — *There is a dog standing at the side of a street a man is crossing. The man is afraid of dogs and fears that the dog will attack him and bite him if he gets any closer. The man starts running in the opposite direction. The dog is now confused and following its instinct, it starts chasing the man, barking loudly. The man runs for some time and then realizes that the dog is gaining on him, getting closer by the second. On an impulse, the man stops, picks up a stone and throws*

*it at the dog. It is now the dog's turn to be afraid. It disappears
into the shadows yelping.*

So you can see – as long as the man was running away
from the dog, the dog chased him, making him more afraid.
But as soon as he decided to stand up and face the dog, the dog
vanished. It is exactly the same case with fear. The moment
you decide to stand up and face it, it disappears, leaving you
free to go chase your dreams.

Consider another, more practical example. Suppose Ishani
works for a multinational company that is going through tough
times. There are rumours that some employees are going to be
laid off. Ishani is afraid that she might be laid off too. She lives
in this fear day and night and as a result loses sleep and peace
of mind. As a result, she is confused and low in confidence in
the work she does and the decisions she makes. Her fear wears
her down to the extent that she starts making mistakes in her
work. If she continues in such a state, her fear is likely to come
true. The organization will have all the reasons to fire her in
case of such a situation. However, Ishani's has demonstrated
a lot of dedication and hard work in the past, and her boss,
Nandita, decides to counsel Ishani. She tells Ishani that she
has full faith in her capabilities and makes her see that even in
this situation, Ishani should simply focus on giving her best,
and leave the rest to fate. This timely advice saves Ishani's position in the company and this demonstration of trust by her
boss gives her confidence to resume her work with full vigor.

In this example, however, Ishani would have gone on and
turned her fear into reality had it not been for the timely inter-
vention of her boss. However, not everyone is blessed with such

thoughtful bosses. A better course of action is to be proactive and face our fear. If our fear of losing our job is keeping us awake at nights, we need to address it. If you have a good relationship with your boss, you can go on and have a candid chat with him/her about the situation. What is the worst that can happen? If the boss is indeed considering firing you, your talking to him will not change his decision. In fact, you may get clarity and can begin planning the next move. However, in case your boss isn't planning to fire you, your fears will be assuaged, and you can continue with your work. However, if you haven't worked with your boss for long enough, and you do not know how your candid discussion will be perceived, it is best to tell yourself that you really do not know what is going to happen. And in such a situation, the most you can do is really just keeping doing your best at your job. But in the meanwhile, you can also start parallel proactive processes such as updating your resume and your professional profile. You can start speaking to your contacts at other organizations and start searching for a suitable opportunity. This way, you can turn this potentially devastating state of affairs into a win-win situation.

This example brings us to an important conclusion. Fear can open up new doors for us. We will look at how this can happen in the next chapter. But for now, remember that fear is not reality. Simply by standing up to your fear and facing it boldly, you can conquer it. As human beings, we can never really be free of fear, but we have to learn to get past it.

Turn Your Fear into an Opportunity

This may sound too good to be true, but our fears can indeed open doors to success. They may help us discover the opportunities that await us. By recognizing our fears, assessing their causes, and deciding how to overpower them, we can actually achieve bigger and better results than we had set out for.

Fear might not be the only reason, but is one of the major reasons why many people miss out on great opportunities. The root cause of fear in our practical life is our feeling of uncertainty, insecurity, and doubts. We are habitual of living within our comfort zone. Anything of value, anything worth doing that's going to make a real impact, often brings up fear. Whenever we do try to start something new, doubts and insecurities rear up in our mind. To combat such thoughts, we have to come out of our comfort zone shedding our fears and doubts. Fear comes as a teacher and if we are open to lessons and can get past our own resisting thoughts, we can make a new beginning and can get exactly what we want.

So far, we have only considered examples where our fears haven't come true. Let us now talk about the worst-case scenario. Suppose our fear does come true. Suppose Ishani does get fired. Suppose your boss is indeed contemplating firing you. What should you do? Should we stop doing whatever we do best simply because what we feared happened? Should we completely lose faith in what we do and how we do it? No, definitely not. However, we should definitely think about what we could have done to avoid it. In fact, this is true even if what you fear hasn't yet happened. You should think about the cause of your fear. Is your self-doubt stemming from a belief that you have indeed not given your best? Are you afraid that you made a mistake and that mistake will be caught? Did you miss something important while doing your job? If this is the case, all is still not lost. If you still have time in your hands, do what is required to be done to ensure that the gaps are well taken care of. And in case there is no time to take corrective action, do an impact analysis to figure out exactly what is the risk. If the risk is huge, make a viable contingency plan and take your seniors into confidence. You will see that once you have taken corrective actions, you will sleep much easier.

Fear is the precursor of possibility. We all feel fear in every area of our life, be it finances, career, relationships, or personal goals. When we wish to attempt something big, important or valuable we usually feel scared, whether it is opening a new office, joining a new post, starting a new business, or joining a partnership firm. With the fear of chasing a big dream also comes the awesome possibility of actualizing that dream.

Who but the legendary Indian mystic poet and saint Kabir Das could have put it in better words:

डर करनी डर परम गुरु, डर पारस डर सार।
डरत रहै सो ऊबरे, ग़ाफ़िल खाई मार।

(Fear makes us work, and is the greatest teacher. It is the Paras Patthar that converts iron into gold. Fear in fact is the essence of everything. Those who feel fear are also the ones who overcome it. Those who are careless, often lose out.)

The Story of Raman and Aman

Raman's dream was to set up a manufacturing unit for decorative tiles. He wanted to supply these to top builders and make a name for himself. He had a diploma in Interior Design and the necessary technical training to understand how tiles are made. However, this was still a herculean task for him. He was short on funds. He didn't have land to set up the unit and also to procure the basic raw material – clay. His parents too were salaried employees with the state government and did not have enough money to spare for Raman's project. He discussed his dream with his friend Aman who agreed to be his partner. Aman, too, was a Civil Engineer and Raman saw value in partnering with him.

Since both were qualified in their respective fields of work, bank agreed to grant them a loan to start their business. They got their unit registered and procured a piece of land for mining clay and clay minerals. With great pomp and show, they inaugurated the unit and started out to achieve their dream.

In the first year of their business, they could hardly save anything because of fixed expenses. In the beginning of the second year, they crossed the break-even point and hoped to start making profits in near future.

But things are usually not this smooth. To their dismay, the land they were using to mine clay turned out to have a bed of solid rock, which couldn't yield any clay. This was an unforeseen obstacle and a rather debilitating one. Clay was the basic raw material they required to keep manufacturing their tiles. Once it ran out, the manufacturing process was halted. As a result, labour was sitting idle and fixed expenditure still kept growing.

They ran into financial problems and were not able to pay the bank's installment or the workers' wages in time. With time the bank and the workers were all getting impatient. Everyone was demanding their dues. Moreover, payments from the retailers too ceased because the supply of tiles had ceased. The machinery had come to a grinding stop.

Raman and Aman were now feeling the heat of the situation. Raman spent many sleepless nights in fear of a legal action against him for failing to repay the Bank loan and the wages of labour. Land Revenue Authorities could get him arrested for not paying the due share of money for mining the clay from their land. Bank could confiscate his parents' house. His employees could drag him to the court.

A scene of horror was created in Raman's mind and he was afraid of losing everything.

He decided to give up on the project. He sold his personal assets to offload some of his financial burden and resigned from the partnership of the project.

The responsibility of running the business now landed on Aman's shoulders. It was up to him whether he wanted to carry on or withdraw like Raman. Aman decided to carry on. He re-designed the entire project and changed his product from decorative tiles to hard roof tiles, which could be made out of the rock dust. He envisioned using new technology-enabled methods to cut the manufacturing costs of his product. He presented his ideas to his Bankers, his clients, retailers, and builders. After having examined his new project, everyone agreed to his point of view. He joined a specialized training institute to get well acquainted with the process of manufacturing roof tiles. After working hard for a period of two years, his company started emerging as a trustworthy brand in roof tiles.

Why did Raman have to give up and from where did Aman get the courage to carry on? Raman let his fear overcome him and took the route that led him out of that worrisome situation. In turn, however, he had to give up on his dreams. Aman on the other hand made his fears his strength. Instead of letting them overcome him, he chose to conquer them. Seeing his courage and his positive outlook under duress, various stakeholders too believed in his capability and courage.

Aman believed in his ability to turn things around, whereas Raman chose not to. Both made their respective choices.

From the above example, it is clear that we must have faith in our own powers. But it is also important to note that our state of mind is like a magnet. If we send out negativity into the Universe, we will get negativity in return. Whatever we think of, whatever we feel, has its own magnetic force. All our feelings like love, fear, anger, happiness, joy, and gratitude etc. create a magnetic pull that attracts actions, plans, and events towards us. Similarly fear of something creates a magnetic force that will attract more of what we fear towards us. This isn't because of any supernatural power. It is common sense.

It is human nature to be concerned about bad situations in our personal, professional, or family life. We worry about situations that are beyond our control. And once we do start worrying, it is like a vortex that sucks us in. It turns our world dark and makes us negative. If you think negative in any situation, you will view everything through the prism of your worry. Even if you achieve success in something, negative mindset will not let you acknowledge it. It will force you to find negativity in positive circumstances too. This is why we see people getting frustrated even when their children score 90 per cent in school exams. This is why we see professionals indulge in gossips in their workplace and end up feeling frustrated even though their careers are going well. This is why we see jealousy in friendships and familial relationships. Because of negativity we fail to feel happy for our friends when they achieve success in their lives.

As our shadow looks larger to us than our physical being and worry gives small things a big shadow. If we have a little problem and worry about it, it will seem a lot worse than it actually is. If something is small let it be small. If we worry about it, we will turn it into something bigger than it is. Let us consider the example for Asha's father.

What is Ailing Asha's Father?

Mr. Vipin Arora, Asha's father, was not feeling well for the last few days and his health was deteriorating consistently. Mr. Arora's wife was very worried about her husband's health. She asked Asha to arrange for him to undergo a medical checkup. Since Asha too was worried she availed the facilities provided by her employers and quickly arranged for a thorough medical checkup at a reputed hospital. However, nothing serious was found. But Mr. Arora's health stayed the same and there was no visible improvement. Asha took him to a homeopathy doctor whose treatment lasted several days. However, this too did not help. Friends then suggested her to take Mr. Arora on a vacation to a quiet, peaceful hill station. Asha did this too. She took her parents to a little hill station. However, even when after a week, Mr. Arora's health did not show any sign of improvement, she decided to bring them back. She was spending too much time away from work and was worried that this would not go down well with her seniors.

On their way back, they stopped at a busy highway food court for lunch. Asha grabbed a table and asked her parents to wait there while she joined the queue to get food. When she came back with the food trays she saw her mother sitting alone at the table. She asked her about her father's whereabouts. Her mother told her that he had gone to the restroom. Mother and daughter waited for some time for Mr. Arora to return but when he wasn't back for a long time, Asha got up to look for her father.

She found him sitting on another table talking to someone. It seemed that he had met someone from their neighborhood there and was happily talking to the person. All signs of illness had vanished from Mr. Arora's face and he seemed to be his jovial self again. They reached home and everyone found that his father had fully recovered from his illness. Nobody knew what his illness was and how he had recovered.

After a few days it was found that Mr. Arora had taken a loan from the neighbor he had met at the food court. Mr. Arora had mortgaged their house without consulting his family members but was not able to pay the last few installments and get the papers back. The neighbor had been pressing him hard for repayment. If the loan was not repaid in time, the neighbor could effectively get them evicted from their house. As a result, Mr. Arora had been avoiding meeting the neighbor for some time.

When he suddenly came across the neighbor at the food court, the neighbor had confronted him about the situation and Mr. Arora was left with no choice but to explain to the neighbor that he will only be able to make the remaining payment after a few months. The neighbor had

understood the problem and told Mr. Arora not to worry
about it so much and it was okay if he repaid the amount
in 6 months. After speaking clearly to the neighbor, Mr.
Arora had become less worried and more relaxed. Realiz-
ing the situation her father was in, Asha repaid the
remaining loan and got the property papers back.

It was nothing but worry that was ailing Mr. Arora. He hadn't taken his family into confidence when he was mortgaging the house. Nor had he confided his worries in them. He constantly kept thinking about the worst that could happen and therefore instead of speaking candidly to the neighbor, he had started avoiding him. This situation had created unwanted stress for him and he hadn't been able to overcome his fear. Perhaps if he had gone ahead and spoken to the neighbor or to his daughter when he was unable to repay the remaining amount, he wouldn't have had any reasons to worry.

Sometimes we fear the things which are not going to happen. Sometimes our own action becomes the cause of fear for ourselves and our family members.

As per motivational public speaker and author Brian Tracy:

"Every time you repeat the words 'I can do it' with
conviction, you override your fear and increase your
confidence. By repeating this affirmation over and over,
you can eventually build your courage and confidence to
the point where you are unafraid."

Ex-President APJ Abdul Kalam has suggested speaking these five lines to ourselves every morning:

I am the best.
I can do it.
God is always with me.
I am a winner.
Today is my day.

If we start our day with positive reaffirmations, we tend to stay charged up throughout the day. Yes, it is true we feel fear and our feelings are part of our life. It is also true our fear is the most powerful single factor that deprives us of being able to achieve our full potential. But there is another factor in our life, our dream and our goal, which inspires us to face all the odds of life, to shed our all fears and continue our journey. The road we are traveling may be a bit scary at times. It's fine to feel a bit uncomfortable. It is okay if we don't know exactly what's going to happen next. As long as we keep stepping forward, we will keep making progress. We overcome the imaginary scary things that might happen and start to see all the great realities unfold around us. It is our life and it's an open road. We must grab the wheel with both hands and keep steering ourselves around all the unnecessary fears and uncertainties as they arise.

To make this point clearer let us consider the example of ants. These tiny creatures keep moving forward without worrying about any imaginary obstacles that may come their way. They deal with obstacles when they actually come face to face with them. And in most cases, even creatures as tiny as ants are able to find their way around the obstacles. We can learn a great deal from these tenacious creatures. These tiny insects demonstrate the main principle of life, the very mantra to success. They teach us to carry on without fear. They teach us that no obstacle is too big and if we do come across it, we will be able to find our way around it.

Avoid the Common Traps

It is one thing to be successful and it is quite another to handle success gracefully. Staying grounded and humble is more difficult than it sounds. Many of us, at the first taste of success, forget what it took to reach here and the people who helped you on the way. This is not only being ungrateful, but it can also be the cause why we cannot stay successful. While how we react to success depends upon our journey in life so far, there are some traps that you can watch out for and learn to avoid so as to stay successful.

EGO

Most people confuse ego with pride, whereas they are two very distinct terms. Let us try to first understand both.

Here are the definitions of both as per the Oxford Online Dictionary.

Ego – A person's sense of self-esteem or self-importance.

Pride – A feeling of deep pleasure or satisfaction derived from one's own achievements, the achievements of one's close associates, or from qualities or possessions that are widely admired.

You can probably see that Ego has its root in a person's perception of the self, whereas Pride stems from the actual work that a person has done and the distance the person has travelled. While Ego can be baseless (after all just because a person feels that he/she is superior to the others, doesn't necessarily make it true), pride often has a strong base. Ego is self-centered, whereas pride can be related to achievements of the others too. Therefore, while one's Ego may come in the way of success, pride usually helps a person succeed. Ego makes a person harsh, whereas Pride makes one humble. Ego makes one arrogant, whereas Pride makes one confident.

Now that we have understood these two terms well, let us explore how ego can cause someone's downfall. Let us look at the story of Mr. Pal.

Mr. Pal and Success

Mr. Pal was the most liked person in his office. It was only six months back when he had joined as an office-assistant in a Bank where everyone was overloaded with work. Due to the heavy burden of work co-workers rarely got time to sit together and share their difficulties. Their immediate Boss, the Branch Manager, always seemed irritated because he was always under tremendous pressure from his bosses. Whenever he needed help with the tasks the Head Office demanded of him, he could hardly find anyone with spare time to help him. In such situations, Mr. Pal was the only one who offered help. And it wasn't only for his Manager; Mr. Pal was always ready to help all of his fellow workers in the branch.

And he did everything with a smile, even if he was tremendously overburdened with work. Never the one to feel angry or irritated, he accepted everything happily and positively. Due to his politeness, humility, cheerfulness, and helpfulness, he was everyone's favorite. And he deserved all the accolades because he was, in fact, a hardworking person, sincere and honest. Due to his personal traits, his services were recognized by higher officers and he was soon promoted to a higher grade. Very soon he was promoted to the post of a General Manager.

When he found himself sitting in the chamber of the General Manager, he felt elevated like a king. A very elegant spacious room, shining furniture, personal staff, chauffeur-driven large and ultra-modern car, fully furnished big residential bungalow, laptop, mobile, free air travel, medical services, were all available to him in the capacity of General Manager. All the lower staff paid him high respect. Whenever he entered the office everyone present would stand up from their seats in his honor. His words were taken as orders.

He thought himself to be a man of high capabilities with extraordinary talent and he felt superior to everyone else.

He thought of himself as the most important person in the organization. He made it a point to criticize everything his juniors did. He found faults with each line of every paragraph of all reports that came to him. "I" and "Me" were of paramount importance to him. According to him, what he did was right, what he thought was proper, what he possessed was the best of all. According to him his opinion was best suited in all situations. He made his own parameters to judge others.

His private secretary was instructed not to allow anybody inside his chamber without his prior permission. One fine morning when his private secretary was not in his seat a gentleman entered Mr. Pal's chamber with some urgent official work. When Mr. Pal saw this intruder, his first reaction was rage. "How dare this man enter my chamber without seeking my permission," he thought. Without bothering to find out the purpose of the man's visit Mr. Pal started rebuking him. The gentleman, bewildered by the arrogant behavior, left Mr. Pal's cabin instantly without talking to him.

In those days, Mr. Pal was working on a presentation for a foreign delegation scheduled to arrive next week, but lacked the required knowledge and was feeling terrible. Being the General Manager, he did not want his lower staff to find out about his lack of knowledge. He, therefore, assigned this job to a group of four persons headed by Mr. Bhalla, the Senior Manager. Mr. Bhalla and his team worked hard day and night for the presentation with the help of Mr. Jolly, a private professional expert.

After assigning the job to his juniors, Mr. Pal was now least interested in gaining the required knowledge.

On the fixed date, Managing Director of the bank introduced Mr. Pal to all the foreign delegates as the main responsible person. Feeling elevated, Mr. Pal talked little about the project and started taking credit for everything, giving an impression that no other staff member was capable enough for such an important assignment. Had he not been there it would not have been possible to finish the task in time.

Members of the delegation were more interested in the project and did not care about Mr. Pal's claims and exaggerations. They raised several questions that needed accurate and precise answers. Since his personal involvement was nil he found it difficult to provide minute details, which were with Mr. Jolly the professional expert. Mr. Jolly was not present at the time and all queries were attended to by Mr. Bhalla, who had worked under the guidance of Mr. Jolly. In fact, the gentleman who had entered the cabin of Mr. Pal without his permission was the professional expert, Mr. Jolly who had come with the final script to help Mr. Pal answer the questions that could be raised by the delegation. But after Mr. Pal had shouted at him, he had left the file with his private secretary with a note "It wouldn't be possible for me to work with Mr. Pal."

At the end, it was clear to the Managing Director that Mr. Pal had not only jeopardized a very important event but had also vandalized cordial relations with Mr. Jolly the eminent professional who had been assisting the bank in all major events. As a result, Mr. Pal was demoted and was transferred to an insignificant post in the rural area.

This story is a reflection on how unearned growth and riches leads to the inflation of ego. We all have our beliefs regarding our personality, talents, abilities which attribute to our skills. But when these beliefs aren't based in reality, they result in an inflated ego.

Shri Sathya Sai Baba has said:

"You are not one person, but three: the one you think you are; the one others think you are; the one you really are."

When we don't need to work hard to achieve success or to earn wealth, the gap between our image of ourselves and our actual selves increases and this gap has the potential to cause our downfall. Mr. Pal in the above story was able to rise to the post of General Manger by the virtue of his qualities of humbleness and was loved and respected by all. As soon as he achieved success too soon in his career, he lost control on his ego and forgot his roots. The very people who had helped him get to where he was meant nothing to him. His behavior towards them and everyone else changed. He was alienated from his actual self and his well-wishers, and this subsequently brought about his downfall.

Over the time, our inflated ego becomes our identity, an identity which is false. Uncontrolled and inflated ego may turn dangerous, lethal, and destructive, probably more than any other negative quality. Ego has brought down more kingdoms, toppled more empires, caused more wars, destroyed more marriages, and ruined more friendships than any other trait in human personality.

In fact, ego keeps us wrapped in a kind of cocoon, oblivious to the world outside our own. It makes us separated by preventing us from seeing the views of other people. It also prevents us from seeing the pain or needs of others. We shall be able to break out of our prison of Ego only if we begin to understand that there is more to this life than our own experience, our own education, our own thinking and start accepting the bare fact that we are all influenced by the actions of those around us.

BEFRIENDING EGO

Everyone has ego, however, it is our responsibility to keep it from overshadowing everything else. And we can do this by "befriending" it.

People say ego works as a foe, not as a friend. If we have Ego, it will make us do all the wrongs. This type of perception has been embedded in our mind, which is not necessarily and completely true. In fact, we all have at least an iota of Ego. This may differ from person to person. Some of us keep our egos deflated and others roam about with their egos inflated.

We all possess our own egos. It is a lesson we all have been reading since our childhood when we were taught to recognize ourselves as a separate entity, responsible for our own successes and failures. We have been taught to be strong enough to compete and fight our way to our success. However, the parameter of success remained undefined or incomplete. Acquisition of wealth and power remained the most preferred parameter of success for most of us. This parameter persuaded us to focus on advancing our personal interest on a priority basis. And this turned out to be the root cause of inflated Ego.

Ego can make us feel different from others. This is nothing more than our urge to cultivate whatever skills, talents, habits and behavior are the most conducive to our success as an individual. So long as it remains within limits, it helps us grow. It becomes a barrier only if it becomes inflated and goes out of our control.

Buddhist literature has dealt with this aspect of Ego in details:

> *"The Ego is only an enemy because it is wild, uncontrolled, and primitive, like many other aspects of the untrained mind. You do not kill a problem dog, you teach it to behave! Do not expect a problem dog to become good if you neglect it and berate it. Without Ego in its most basic form, it is impossible to have any desire, make any decision, have any awareness, or possess any of the critical qualities of a humanely developed person."*

It is very hard to destroy one's Ego absolutely as it is an essential component of our personality, but we must strive hard to control it and purify it of the impurities that tarnish our image, our conscience, and our experience. We should learn to master our Ego before it takes charge of our life. Once Ego takes charge of us we close our eyes, hearts, inner conscience in situations when we think our personal interests are at stake.

Much like GPS, our ego is supposed to guide us safely to our destination. But if we have programmed our GPS with vested personal interests, it may not serve our purpose. In that case, it would be worse than useless. Not only would it fail to help us reach our destination, it will completely mislead us – which is exactly what our ego is doing. Not because it is inherently evil or malicious but because it is relying on incorrect information. Our task then is to reprogram our ego so that it can more effectively fulfill its mission of protecting us. Reprogramming means befriending our ego.

When we befriend our Ego it would serve us to nourish our self-esteem and to achieve our goals. We can benefit from our Ego when we are the one controlling it. Befriending Ego does not mean getting away from our most important component of life but to just modify it in a way so that is true to our real self and is humbler to others who helped pave a path to success for us. Modifying our Ego or befriending it leaves us to use its strength for more creative purposes. It is like clay in the hands of a potter who can mould it into many different shapes suitable for us, but its essence will remain the same. It is still the clay, all the different shapes he made are still just the clay and they may look different and friendlier. Likewise, we can shape and reshape our ego so that it serves the purpose of guiding us.

Ultimately, the aim should be to have a healthy, functional, content and loving Ego which explores the spirit of life. Expand it, empower it, enlighten it. It should also have a balanced attachment to itself, which means it should be attached to the purpose that is practical for its existence but not attached in ways that reinforce pain and sufferings to itself and others.

To understand this further, consider the following example of how Mir Mohammad Ali Khan, the internationally acclaimed investment banker, realized his dreams.

Mir Mohammad Ali Khan and his Ego

At the age of 19 years, Mir Mohammad Ali Khan landed in America. Initially he was overwhelmed by the shock of a new culture, unfamiliar faces and people, and a completely different way of life. While he was hunting for a job, he came across a signboard at Burger King "HELP WANTED, APPLY WITHIN". He just walked in and met the Manager named John Reid. After a short interview, he was offered the job @ 3.55 dollars an hour. His duty chart included cleaning tables, mopping the restaurant floor, and cleaning Bathrooms as well.

A chill went down his spine. He belonged to a royal family. His paternal grandfather was the Royal Mir of Deccan. His maternal Grandfather was the Governor of 5 Provinces. His house in Karachi, Pakistan, was swarming with servants, who were happy to do whatever they were asked to do. His ego was prompting him to reject the offer. However, he was also painfully aware that he had come to America with a goal. He needed money to attend University. Refusing the job would shatter his dream. He thought for a while about his royal stature and his present position as well as his future plans. Without wasting any more time he accepted the job, shedding his ego. This was the moment which could have stopped his ascent in

America to own an Investment bank on Wall Street had he not befriended his ego.

Every morning he would walk 4 miles from his sister's house through knee-high snow to get to the Burger King. The first day when he was mopping the floor wearing the common Burger King Uniform, he started crying, thinking about what his life had come down to. When his manager asked why he was weeping, he hid his emotions and said that it was because of ammonia in his bucket, which was irritating his eyes.

The first thing he learned was that when life deals us a hand that we do not like, take it and make the best out of it. He had set a goal and his goal was to make money to pay his university fee. He could not succumb to the pressure of ego. He just wanted to focus on his goals. He would work there until 4 pm and take his full-time classes from 5.45 to 11.45 at night. On Saturdays and Sundays, he would work at a Corporate Security Desk from 7 in the morning till 11 at night. 16 hours on Saturday and Sunday provided him enough time to study because hardly any employees came in on the weekends. He, in fact, had found a job where he could earn money as well as continue with his studies. Next year he drove a Taxi from Summer County to New York Airport facing all kinds of passengers – rude, happy, arrogant, irritated, and obnoxious – you name them and he had them. At such a young age, he learned that one needs to make a house using the same bricks that are thrown at him.

He learned that we should keep our eyes on the goal and not on the ground. He learned so much about the Burger King's operations that later when he was running the Investment Bank and was looking for high-profile American billionaires to sit on his Board of Directors, he met Joe Antonius, Chairman of the 32-billion-dollar conglomerate. The first thing they had in common was that Antonius ran that corporation where Mir once cleaned bathrooms. He went up to him, introduced himself, "Hi Joe! I am Mir Mohammad Ali Khan, founder and Chairman of KMS Investment Bank and my first job in America was washing bathrooms at one of your restaurants." Joe burst out laughing and all top notch people – Bill Gates, Warren Buffet, and Peter Lynch – could not believe what the young man was saying.

Joe took him aside and said, "Tell me honestly what did you like about cleaning bathrooms."

"Ammonia," replied Mir.

"Why?"

Mir said, "I hated my job and it hurt my ego. I hated it so much that I cried throughout the first week and every time somebody saw me crying, I would tell them that it was because of ammonia. Ammonia helped me shelter my ego." Later Antonius joined the Board of Mir's bank for NO COMPENSATION and also brought 6 top people from Forbes, Yoblon, Mario, Andretti, and others. In the first meeting of the Board Antonius said, "I joined this board because if this immigrant kid can come from a family background that he has, compromise with his ego, wash bathrooms and smile and tell us in a corporate meeting of leaders that he is proud of it, then it means that he will go far in life. At 29 he owns a bank, imagine what he will do at 49." Mir Mohammad Ali Khan is now internationally renowned Investment Banker, Entrepreneur & Capital Markets Adviser. Founder and Chairman of a Financial Group, Federal Advisor to the Govt. of Pakistan, a Member of New Jersey State mayors and US State Senators. (Story told by Junaid Tahir)

We usually are always at war with our mind when we find that our ego guides us strongly about what should or shouldn't happen in our life. On one side our mind cultivates ideas of appearing successful, loving, adorable, and desirable, but at the same time, it also resists undesirable results. In such a state we are not able to critically examine the ideas of our mind. Gripped in our mind's one-sided ideas we mostly act unreasonably. On the other side, when we get our peace of mind we are more conscious of what the mind is thinking. This peace of mind allows us to get rid of ridiculous thoughts that inflate our ego.

INFERIORITY COMPLEX

Inferiority complex is the lack of self-esteem and self-confidence, and is characterized by the abundance of self-doubt, uncertainty, and the feeling of not measuring up to standards. When such feelings take over a person's life and prevent him/her from functioning normally, then it can be termed as inferiority complex. Generally speaking, an inferiority complex develops when we feel that everyone around us is better than us in every aspect and that we do not measure up to them. It is the general feeling of not being 'up to the mark'. It stems from low self-esteem, which makes us assume we will fail at everything we do. This makes it hard for us to try new things or complete tasks. This can prevent us from living our life the way we want and can also lead to frustration and depression. Sometimes even when we get a chance to use our talent, we hesitate to perform in high visibility areas for unknown reasons. Something tells us that we cannot pull it off. We cannot identify from where these negative thoughts are originating but these thoughts prevent us from giving our best. And when we are unable to perform well, we often give up on a task without completing it. This is because of inferiority complex and low self-esteem.

Let us consider the example of Prachi and Swati, who were classmates.

Prachi and Swati and the Interview

Prachi got a call to appear in an interview for a post for which she had applied some time ago. She was a good student and had completed her graduation with respectable marks. Happy to have received the invitation, she started preparing hard so that she may come through successful in the proposed interview. She started studying relevant books and notes and even joined a prestigious institute that imparted interview training to prospective candidates from her field. Burning midnight oil, putting in every possible effort, she was feeling very confident by the time the date of the interview was upon her.

On the scheduled date and time, she reached the venue fully prepared. There were a number of other candidates who had also been invited to appear for the same interview. Before the interview started, candidates got into discussions among themselves about their respective qualifications and experiences. Prachi listened attentively all of them. To her dismay, everyone else appeared more qualified than her. They spoke better English than her and many had also passed with higher percentage than her. This discouraged her and within minutes she had forgotten how much hard work she had put in to prepare herself for the interview.

In the meantime, another candidate joined them. Prachi recognized her as Swati, her classmate from school. She was delighted to see her old friend there. A familiar face amongst a sea of unfamiliar ones gave her some comfort. But as soon as they got talking Prachi started noticing how well-dressed Swati was, what an expensive smartphone she was carrying, how neatly her folder was organized, and how easily she smiled. Whatever joy Prachi felt upon seeing Swati disappeared in no time and her nervousness increased. She worried that Swati would land the job instead of her and the fear of everyone finding out that Swati was better than her made her panic. She feigned feeling unwell and left without facing the interview as she was sure of her failure. She did not want others to find out that she was no good. She thought it was better to say that she chose health over her job than to admit defeat.

A week later, Swati came to meet Prachi at her residence to find out how she was feeling now and whether she had recovered from her sudden illness. Prachi avoided the questions about her health but wanted to find out the outcome of the interview. She was sure that despite her better grooming, Swati too would not have made it because everyone else was so much more qualified. To her dismay though, Swati told her that indeed she had appeared for the interview and had cleared it. Prachi was now very sure that Swati had been selected because of her expensive clothes and smartphone. But it turned out that the company was looking for fresh graduates who could be molded according to the company's culture and was looking for qualified but simple and grounded people. The interview board was not concerned about the ranks of candidates but was more interested in their ability, humility, and flexibility. Prachi now felt devastated. She had lost the chance to land up a good job only because she imagined herself to be inferior from everyone else. She confided in Swati and was surprised to find that even Swati, with her expensive clothes and gadgets, had felt nervous at the venue of the interview. However, she had decided to take her chance because she did not have anything to lose by appearing for the interview. In fact, even if she did not land up the job, she would still gain the experience of an interview. She had evaluated it to be a win-win situation for her. In the end, it was Swati's positive attitude that had landed her the job and not her expensive clothes and smartphone.

Upon hearing this, Prachi decided that she had lost this opportunity not because she wasn't qualified for it,

but because of her lack of belief in herself. She had learnt
an important lesson and said heartfelt thanks to Swati for
her insights.

All of us feel inferior in some situation or the other. A college student may feel inferior to his/her classmates. A clerk may feel inferior to his boss. A manager may feel that everyone who reports to him/her is better off because they hail from richer families. Even a millionaire may feel inferior to his less wealthy friends because he/she isn't that good looking. This feeling is common and is usually not harmful. It becomes harmful when we let it define us. When we feel inferior and it starts reflecting in the way we talk to others, the way we behave, and in the decisions we take, it is then that the trouble begins.

Inferiority complex crops up when we feel that we have landed an opportunity by fluke. It occurs when we feel that we do not deserve to be where we are. It may not necessarily be true. At times, we work hard to reach somewhere, but when we reach there we forget what it took to get here and start believing that it was all good luck. Without giving ourselves credit for transcending our physical, intellectual, societal, and financial boundaries, we start doubting whether we indeed deserve the outcome.

There can be other scenarios too. When it comes to setting goals, we aim as high as possible. For example, an entrepreneur may start with the goal of becoming a very successful businessman owning multinational companies with its offices in a number of countries. This goal is not so simple, and it would probably take years of patience and hard work, and would also require a lot of financial investment and creating and leveraging a large network of contacts. Once you are through the initial hurdles, this also requires time to develop infrastructure, to identify and employ skilled workers, to seek various permissions from the authorities, and to fulfill legal formalities. The entire process would take a long time and we will need to grapple uncertainty till we achieve our goal. If during this time of struggle we keep looking at established enterprises and see how far ahead they are when compared to us, we are sure to find ourselves feeling inferior to the others.

Sometimes we also invite inferiority complex when we are not really making the maximum use of our talent, our strengths, and our thoughts. For example, if we are capable, qualified, and trained to work as a senior lecturer in a college, but for the time being because of lack of opportunities, we have to accept a lower position. If we do not learn to deal with this situation and aren't able to land the job that we deserve, there are chances that we will end up losing confidence in our ability and this situation is ripe for inferiority complex to crop up.

When we get caught in the web of inferiority complex, it soon starts manifesting itself in the way we behave. When we are sure that we are inferior to everyone else around us, we start using other tactics to conceal our inferiority. We try to sound confident, without really feeling confident. We may try to emulate others who we feel are better than us. Some may try to feign being rich by buying expensive clothes and gadgets when we aren't really that well off. These steps may work for some time but will be hollow and fall flat at the first obstacle. This attempt to hide our inferiority complex may make us temperamental and insecure. If by chance we happen to get promoted to a position of responsibility with our inferiority complex, the people reporting to us bear the brunt of our insecurities. We try to put undue pressure on them to get the desired results in order to prove that we are good with what we do.

Some scholars are of the view that inferiority complex may stem from our childhood. At times without even realizing this, parents sow the seeds of low self-esteem in their children. It isn't only about being strict with them, it is also about other subtle actions such as comparing our child to other children, using negative statements when talking about our child, or by not demonstrating faith in their ability to achieve things. Most parents don't even realize that children who are at an impressionable age are very sensitive to these subtle signals. And these early impressions are imprinted on their sub-conscious mind. Even when the child grows up, it may take him or her several years of hard work to overcome the damage inflicted during the childhood. In fact, some people never really fully recover from this.

Let us also try to investigate what makes us believe that if we lack some skills that others possess, we are inferior to them. This, in fact, is a deep-rooted problem in our society. While we are not going to propose any solution to this, we are definitely going to discuss how one can deal with this and not let it impact us and our lives.

In our society, it is generally accepted that people who are richer, more beautiful, fairer, slimmer, taller, better communicators etc are superior to the rest. It is our instinct to assume that these people are better in every way when compared to the rest. We not only admire these people, we also look down upon people who do not meet these criteria.

We have grown up watching this unfold all around us. We hardly pay any attention to the beggars on the street, we do not respect our house-help. We make fun of people for the way they look, speak, walk. On the other hand, if we happen to meet a diplomat or successful business person, we go all out to make pleasantries with them. We try our best to develop contacts with them and so on. We pay respect to such people, even at the cost of disrespecting someone less privileged. We feel inferior to the successful people and superior to those who are less successful than us. We have been brought up with these perceptions of hierarchy.

Therefore, a sense of inferiority is practically always present in all of us with our fears and doubts that are cause of our agony. When we look at ourselves with doubt, when we lose our trust in our talent and abilities, it becomes extremely difficult for us to think in daring and exciting ways. Losing our confidence and conviction makes us feel inferior. If we let our feelings of inferiority scare us from thinking, then we will again be obstructed even though we may have the most productive mind in the world.

Inferiority complex is not our weakness but a way of thinking and a psychological condition which can be imposed upon anyone if he is continuously and constantly reminded of it. A genius can come to believe that he is inferior if his faults are pointed out endlessly and he is given no credit or encouragement for his achievements. There is no one on the earth capable of doing everything correctly without faults. If his faults are picked up only for derogatory discussion without taking into consideration his achievements, it is certainly going to make him or her feel inferior.

No matter how hard we try, there will always be someone better than us. So there really is no end to this vicious cycle of comparisons. In fact, this has even been the subject for many stories. Consider the following for example:

The Happy Crow

Once upon a time, there lived a crow in a forest. This crow was absolutely satisfied and happy with its life. One day it happened to go to a pond to drink water. It looked at its reflection in the water and turned its face this way and that. It preened its wings and thought about how shiny they were. The crow was convinced of its beauty. But then he saw a white swan swim by. Some ducks standing near the pond laughed at the crow for its black color and complimented and praised the swan. The crow was full of admiration for the swan. He told the swan that it was beautiful and also added, "you must be the happiest bird in the world."

The swan, however, did not appear so happy. When the crow asked her the reason the swan replied, "I also thought that I was the most beautiful and the happiest bird around, until I saw the parrot. You will not believe it. You and I have just one color, but the parrot has two, green and red. In my opinion, the parrot must be the happiest bird in the world." The crow was intrigued and went to meet the parrot. When he saw the parrot, he too was convinced that it was indeed the most beautiful bird in the forest. When the crow asked the parrot, "you must be the happiest bird in the forest," the parrot laughed and said,

"I too lived under the same illusion, until I saw the peacock. You won't believe how beautiful the peacock is. I have never seen a more colorful bird." The inquisitive crow now went to meet the peacock and indeed it was the most colorful bird anyone could imagine. It danced happily with its wings spread and the crow watched mesmerized.

However, a bird catcher hiding in the bush too had the same reaction and he captured the colorful peacock. The colorful parrot and the white swan too could not escape this fate. However, the crow with its shiny feathers and lustrous wings escaped this fate. The society's bias against dark color saved the crow. The peacock, parrot, and swan looked at the crow flying about freely and thought "this must be the happiest bird in the world."

This is our problem too. We keep comparing ourselves to everyone around us and keep undervaluing our own merits and achievements. Everyone is unique and everyone is beautiful. We must take pride in our own talents, qualities, and strengths, and try to make the best use of them. If we really admire someone for a characteristic they possess, we must appreciate it but this does not mean that we should start feeling inferior simply because we do not possess those qualities.

As per the writer Henry C. Link:

> *"While one person hesitates because he feels inferior, another is busy making mistakes and becoming superior."*

Even if someone else is better than us at something, instead of despairing and retreating into a shell, we must explore our own strengths and be proud of what we possess. When we are comfortable in our own skin, we look beautiful on the outside, regardless of how many flaws we have.

Someone has rightly said:

"The fastest runner doesn't always win the race and the strongest warrior doesn't always win the battle."

The wise sometimes go hungry, and the skillful are not necessarily wealthy. And those who are educated don't always lead successful lives. It takes much more than just one quality to make one successful. And if you are really determined, you will make it despite any lack of skills or ability.

ANGER

All of us are familiar with anger. In fact, at some point or the other in our lives we have faced anger. We have either already bore the brunt of someone's anger or have suffered because of our own anger. With changing of lifestyles, unregulated working, sleeping, and eating hours, stress, lack of free time, and cut-throat competition, anger is becoming more and more common. At the smallest of excuses, we not only become angry, we also let our anger escalate into rage, and rage into violence. Road rage is a manifestation of this issue. An increase in crimes of passion is also a result of this quick temper.

However, anger is not necessarily all bad. In fact, anger is natural to a human being. It is an instinctive response to situations that we do not want to be in or situations that are contrary to our beliefs. Anger comes more easily to us than we imagine. We do not need to face a huge incident or suffer a huge loss to become angry. Children's mischief, boss's demands, house help's unplanned leave, crash of our computer, laziness of our spouse, anything and everything can make us feel irritated. And irritation is a form of anger. We become irritated when we are stuck in a traffic jam, we become irritated when we are standing in a queue, we become irritated when it is too hot, we become irritated when it rains for too long. This irritation adds up and leads to a situation where our anger can flare up at any point.

We may be rightful with our anger in some situations but many times we also feel guilty that we lost our temper. We feel that we could have handled the situation better and accomplished more if we hadn't lost control. It isn't that we do not understand the consequences of uncontrolled anger, but despite knowing and understanding everything, we get angry with people we care for and love.

Anger, its cause, manifestation, and impact have interested many philosophers and psychologists.

The great thinker Swami Vivekanand has said this about anger:

"Good works are continually being undone by the tons of hatred and anger which are being poured out on the world."

And we are seeing this unfold all around us today. Anger has the potential to cause devastation. It has the potential to cause unforeseen miseries. If left unchecked, it can destroy relationships, careers, families, and communities. The following verse of *Bhagavad Gita* explains how and why our anger is the fundamental cause of all sorts of failures in our lives.

क्रोधाद्भवति सम्मोहः सम्मोहात्स्मृति विभ्रमः
स्मृतिभ्रंशाद् बुद्धिनाशो बुद्धिनाशत्प्रणश्यति।

(It is due to anger that a person becomes delusional. As soon as the delusion takes over, his mind loses the power to discern right from wrong. An angry person is unable to control his reactions. When we are angry, our mind is unable to weigh the pros and cons of an action, a question, or a situation. An angry person does not care about the consequences of whatever he/she does in a fit of rage. Under the influence of delusion, people forget what they should and should not do, how they had planned to do something and how they are actually doing it. An angry person loses his/her capability to work as per a predetermined plan. When the mind is clouded with delusion, the reasoning capabilities of a person are lost. A person who cannot reason justly is destined to be doomed. In such a state of mind, he/she can demonstrate hostility, harshness, malice, and foolishness. These reactions can result in terrible consequences and make a person regret his/her actions. Thus, anger is the fundamental cause of all sorts of failures in a person's life.)

Or as the famous writer Mark Twain said:

"Anger is an acid that can do more harm to the vessel in which it is stored than to anything on which it is poured."

Mr. Popli and his Temper

It was winter and Delhi was covered in the blanket of fog. This was the coldest January in decades and it was getting increasingly difficult to wake up early in the morning and get out of the bed. Mr. Popli was no different. One morning, he woke up very late and realized that he would be late for his office. He got out of his bed in panic and rushed about doing his daily chores – using the restroom, taking bath, getting dressed. As it happens when one is in a hurry, these things took longer than usual. With every passing minute, Mr. Popli's temper rose.

Mrs. Popli had been requesting him to purchase some groceries on his way back from office, but day after day he kept forgetting it. Today she had prepared a list so that he wouldn't forget. But before she could hand over the list to him, she saw him fuming around, fumbling with things, getting angrier and angrier. She saw that he was probably going to rush out without having breakfast. She thought that it would be disastrous to try and hand over the list to him in this state. So she stood aside.

When Mr. Popli saw his wife standing with a list in her hands, he assumed that she was again going to remind him to bring the groceries. He was already angry and this irritated him further. He roughly pushed her out of his way, snatched the list, tore it into a hundred pieces, and threw the pieces at her. Mumbling abuses of various kinds, he stormed out of the house, slamming the main door shut behind him.

Unfortunately, this was also the day when the Vice-President was supposed to visit the office for an important meeting. Mr. Popli drove like a madman and still reached office 20 minutes late. Sitting in his cabin, feeling fatigued for reasons not known to him, he was clenching his jaws. A moment later he started grinding his teeth. He wondered what had gone wrong and when he wasn't able to figure out, his frustration grew. After downing glass full of water, he looked for the file he would need to carry to the meeting and remembered that he had left it at home. He started rubbing his temples and pulling at his hair. Not able to start any work he just started doodling on the papers on his table.

One of his juniors noted his unusual body language and sensed that there was something wrong with Mr. Popli. Out of concern for Mr. Popli, the young man went inside his office and saw that Mr. Popli was clenching his fists. The young man asked, "Mr. Popli, are you Okay?"

Mr. Popli did not respond.

The young man asked again, "Sir, are you okay?"

Mr. Popli simply stared at the young man and did not respond.

Sensing some serious issue, the young man persisted. He went closer and asked again, "Sir, are you okay?"

Mr. Popli stood up from his seat, slammed is palms on the table, picked up the heavy, glass paperweight and hurled it with full force towards the young man enquiring about his well-being. Luckily the young man was quick and he was intuitive enough to judge the actions of Mr. Popli.

However, the Vice President standing behind the young man wasn't so lucky. The young man ducked in time and the paperweight caught the Vice President in the center of his forehead. The Vice President fell down and started bleeding. Mr. Popli suddenly woke up from his trance and realized what had just happened. However, he could not roll back his actions. It was too late.

Over time, the Vice President recovered and resumed his job. The young man though shocked was unaffected. However, Mr. Popli could not escape unhurt. He was fired from his job for causing grievous injury to a senior official and for unprofessional conduct and irresponsible attitude.

What Mr. Popli didn't realize was that all his rage was for nothing. He didn't realize that everyone was trying to help him – his wife by preparing the list and then deciding not to hand it over to him, the young man by enquiring about his well-being. Instead Mr. Popli saw himself as a victim and let a situation that was already in his control get out of control. As someone wise has said:

"A matchstick before burning other things burns itself. Our anger is also like a matchstick. Before destroying others, it destroys us."

Mr. Popli's irritation started when he woke up late in the morning. He was worried about getting late for his office. But instead of thinking of ways to cope with the situation, he kept trying to hurry through his daily chores and kept getting more and more irritated as things took longer than expected.

If he had sat down and thought about the situation, there were several ways out of it. He could have called up his office and informed that he was going to be a little late. He could have got his breakfast packed, he could have requested his wife to help with ironing clothes, and searching for a matching tie. Instead he kept trying to do everything himself.

He took his frustration right up to his office where he reached late. Here was another chance for him to deal with his frustration with a cool mind. But he failed again. He did not try to cool down. He did not try to think what could be done when he realized that he had forgotten the file at home. Instead he misbehaved with the young man. Only a violent incident, his paperweight hurting the Vice President jolted him out of his madness.

Had he controlled his irritation, frustration, and anger in time he would have realized that his concerned wife had already informed the office on the phone of his being late and having forgotten his file at home, and consequently the Vice-President had already managed to get the file picked up from his house. Everything had already been arranged for the success of the scheduled important meeting but because of Mr. Popli's uncontrolled anger, everything was lost.

But it isn't only the common man who suffers the consequences of anger. Even saints are wary of the wrath of anger.

Here is the story of Swami Vivekanand's anger. In his early days, Swami Vivekanand was also famous for his short temper. Over time he learnt that while demonstrating anger can yield unfortunate consequences, controlling and channeling it can work wonders. He has also shared some insights into how one can control his/her anger.

Swami Vivekanand and his Anger

"When I am angry, my whole mind becomes a huge wave of anger. I feel it, see it, handle it, can easily manipulate it, can fight with it; but I shall not succeed perfectly in the fight until I can get down below to its causes. A man says something very harsh to me, and I begin to feel that I am getting heated, and he goes on till I am perfectly angry and forget myself, identify myself with anger. When he first began to abuse me, I thought, "I am going to be angry". Anger was one thing, and I was another; but when I became angry, I was anger. These feelings have to be controlled in the germ, the root, in their fine forms, before even we have become conscious that they are acting on us. With the vast majority of mankind the fine states of these passions are not even known – the states in which they emerge from sub consciousness. When a bubble is rising from the bottom of the lake, we do not see it, nor even when it is nearly come to the surface; it is only when it bursts and makes a ripple that we know it is there. We shall only be successful in grappling with the waves when we can get hold of them in their fine causes, and until you can get hold of them, and subdue them before they become gross, there is no hope of conquering any passion perfectly. To control our passions we have to control them at their very roots; then alone shall we be able to burn out their very seeds. As fried seeds thrown into the ground will never come up, so these passions will never arise."

We have explored the destructive side of anger so far. But like fire that has the power to destroy as well as the power to create, anger too is a very powerful emotion that destroys as well as creates.

Before we get angry we normally first feel afraid, attacked, offended, disrespected, forced, trapped, or pressurized. These are ignition points that lead us into a fit of anger. If these points are not regulated as soon as they spur we get entrapped in the state of anger. We must remember that all these ignition points are indications for us to prepare ourselves for proactive actions, so that we can utilize our anger in the best possible way.

In fact, anger is the sure shot sign that something is wrong, and not necessarily with you. It means that something needs to change, either within or outside.

Remember, all our fits of anger are not inappropriate or destructive. If we express our anger in a controlled and respectful way, it can be appropriate and effective. It can help us to take action, solve problems, or to better deal with situations at hand. It may help us in many ways.

Regulated anger may help us express ourselves in a forceful yet respectful manner. Anger makes us feel stronger and for a while we are not afraid. We start feeling as if we are in charge and as long as we control our speech and body language, a little anger can get us great results.

With changing times, it is becoming more and more important to be assertive, if not aggressive. If you are a quiet person, someone who does not want to raise his/her voice, you will find that it is becoming increasingly difficult to be heard in a group of people. Also, if you get angry when someone is being unreasonable or when someone is trying to take advantage of you, and you are brave enough to express your displeasure in a loud voice, chances are that people would stop thinking of you as an easy target.

In the words of Aristotle:

> *"The man who is angry at the right things and with the right people, and, further, as he ought, when he ought, and as long as he ought, is praised."*

The Monk and the Boat

A monk decides to meditate alone for some time. From his monastery, he takes a boat and sets sail in it on the lake. When he reaches the middle of the lake, he moors the boat there. He closes his eyes and starts meditating. After a few hours of undisturbed silence, he suddenly feels a bump of another boat colliding into his own. With his eyes still closed, he senses his anger rising, and by the time he opens his eyes, he is ready to scream at the boatman who dared to disturb his meditation. But when he opens his eyes, he sees that it was in fact an empty boat that had probably got untethered and floated to the middle of the lake. At that moment the monk achieves self-realization and understands that the anger is actually within him. It really just needs the bump of an external object to provoke it out of him. From then on, whenever he came across someone who irritated him or provoked him and made him angry, he reminded himself, "The other person is merely an empty boat. The anger is within me."

In reality, we all have the anger with us, all the time. All it needs is someone or something like an empty boat to provoke it.

Harvest the Power of Thoughts

With all the advancements in the various fields of science, our understanding of thoughts is sadly limited. We do not exactly know how thoughts originate in our brain. We do, however, know that they help us make sense of the world. In general, thoughts can belong to the following three categories:

1. ## Pathological Thoughts

   These are spontaneous thoughts that mostly result from an emotion. This emotion can be either negative or positive. A lot of this type of thinking happens at the subconscious level and only a few of these thoughts make it to our conscious mind.

2. Logical Thoughts

Logical thoughts usually arise when we are trying to solve a problem. These are results of deliberate thinking.

3. Psychological Thoughts

Psychological thoughts are self-evaluating. They help you question and understand yourself, your own actions, reactions and relationships.

We can only control what goes on in our conscious mind and that too to a limited extent. What goes on in our subconscious mind is largely invisible to us. However, with a bit of practice we can harvest the power of our subconscious mind too, if not control it.

Thoughts are seeds, and as the old proverb goes – as we sow, so shall we reap.

None other than Mahatma Gandhi himself has said:

"A man is but the product of his thoughts – what he thinks, he becomes."

If we spare a minute and look at our lives, we will find it to be a reflection of our thoughts. We think about everything. This includes dreams of becoming rich, worry about our weak financial conditions. We have thoughts about health, illness, safety, risk, fear, violence. We also fear society's judgment of us and the prospect of losses and sorrow. We worry about our professional growth, our retirement, our children's future, our parents' health. There is no limit to our thoughts. We do not know how or from where we get these thoughts. However, we do know that these thoughts often lead to some action. And, therefore, thoughts work as a source of power.

A very famous quote, attributed to many great thinkers, goes something like this:

> *"When you sow a thought you reap an action, when you sow an action you reap a habit, when you sow a habit you reap a character and when you sow a character you reap a destiny. Thoughts are like seeds. You cannot sow the seed of one plant and get another: thistles will never produce daffodils! When your thoughts are positive, powerful, and constructive, your life will reflect this."*

However, such is the state of things that sitting down and thinking actively is no longer considered a productive way to spend your time. We focus too much on action, and not so much on thoughts.

If we think about disaster, we are more likely to get disaster. If we think about something good, we will most probably get something good. Whatever we think manifests itself in some form or the other. If we think positive, with confidence and faith, our life will become more secure, more fraught with action, richer in achievement and experience. Our thoughts must always be positive and high in ideals.

Our thoughts can also influence our dreams, even though at times the connection might not seem too apparent. On most nights, our dreams don't make sense to us but we often see people we have met during the day and things that have happened through the day in some form in our dreams.

At times we aren't even aware that we were thinking about these people or events, but our subconscious was obviously keeping busy. Let us try to understand this with the help of an anecdote.

Mulla Nasruddin in Paradise

Once the famous Mulla Nasruddin was thinking about what facilities and comforts might be available in paradise. He reached paradise in his dreams and saw amazing royal abundance of everything easily available to everyone. In paradise, he found that all his wishes were being fulfilled just by thinking about them. He felt hungry and craved delicious food, and lo and behold, a table full of different dishes that he was thinking about appeared right before him.

Wow! He was surprised. It appeared to be a miracle to have such sumptuous food just by thinking about it. However, his practical mind made him question the possibility of food materializing out of nowhere simply because he had thought about it. And immediately the table topped up with food disappeared. He repented his cynicism and desired the food back. The dishes appeared again. He finished the food and now craved something to drink. Immediately, the wine that he liked the best appeared and he was delighted.

After consuming heavy food and wine he felt sleepy and thought he needed to lie down for a bit. While taking rest he wondered about the one who was arranging all this luxury in paradise. This definitely cannot be the doing of any human being. There must be some other force behind it. May be it was ghosts, he thought. And suddenly, he was surrounded by ghosts. They were terrible and looked exactly like he had imagined them. Mulla Nasruddin was scared of the ghosts and thought that they would throw him out of the paradise. The ghosts immediately grabbed him by his legs and threw him out of the paradise.

Upon waking up from his reverie, Mulla told his wife that everyone lives in a world created by his thoughts and gets what he deserves.

This is more than just a fun story. If you take out the magic and the exaggeration, you will see that it actually is a commentary on how things happen in our life too.

While there is no scientific proof that our thoughts reflect in our life, there are many theories. You have probably experienced this some time. Imagine that you are carrying a tray with a glass full of water to serve to your guest. If you keep worrying that you will spill the water, chances are that you will spill some. However, if you confidently keep walking, chances are that you will make it to the guest without spilling any water.

Now consider another example. You were scheduled to reach office in time for an urgent meeting with your boss, but somehow you got late. You pray hard for a way out of the soup that you are definitely going to be in. Upon reaching the office, you find that the boss can't make it to office and is on leave. He has dropped you an email expressing his regret at having to postpone the meeting. You can't believe your luck but are definitely relieved that your prayers have been answered.

Out of the two examples above, the first one can probably be considered a case of thoughts altering our state of mind and hence making us nervous. This may have then led to us spilling the water. The second example can probably be pure good luck. However, our thoughts are indeed the first step that makes us creative in our actions. It is up to us to ensure that we gear up our thoughts and train them to go in the right direction. Our thoughts are very powerful and may determine the final outcome. In other words, what we think will, in the end, produce the result we think about. It can be good and it can be bad. It depends on us.

We are living in the world of advanced technology where many scientists, inventors, and thinkers have created or invented great things to make our life better. All these inventors had one single thing in common. Their inventions came from one thought. The most advanced gadgets that we use to make our life easy emerged from thoughts which have become reality now. For centuries, humanity had been thinking of a possibility of humans being able to fly. And after concentrated thinking and actions in this direction, we made airplanes that are now such integral parts of our life. And it all started with a thought.

The invention of the telephone has been possible because of one thought of Alexander Grahm Bell and his subsequent actions. In the absence of telephone, we might have still being using primitive forms of communication.

We cannot imagine living in a world without electricity. Had Benjamin Franklin not followed his single thought with action, we would never have discovered electricity.

A wise person once said that thoughts create things. So, if thoughts are so powerful, imagine what they can do if we use them in the right way and follow them up with solid logical thinking, planning, and execution. Be not afraid, if a single thought has not worked we should think again and go on thinking till we get the right path.

Essayist Henry David Thoreau has said:

"As a single footstep does not make a path on the earth, so a single thought will not make a pathway in the mind. To make a deep physical path, we walk again and again. To make a deep mental path, we must think over and over the kind of thoughts we wish to dominate our lives."

Imagine our lives without The Internet. Had Leonard Kleinrock not thought of paving a path towards development of this communication technology we still would have been waiting for weeks to get our post. No doubt it wasn't a single thought of one single person that led to this. It took the abilities of many others like J.C.R. Licklider and Robert Taylor to bring about this miracle. The creation of Internet gave Tim Berners-Lee the idea of making WORLD WIDE WEB, which is now popularly known and written as WWW.

Behind the wireless communication, there is that first thought of Martin Cooper who invented mobile phone, a handset device that has brought our loved ones so close that we can talk to them while lying down in our bed, no matter where they are in the world.

Similarly, we can also create what we think about. We are equipped with immense power of thoughts that are full of imagination and, therefore, promise. But this requires us to be very responsible too. Don't let your mind think of things you do not want to bring to this world or to yourself. Your thoughts effect your state of mind so be careful what you think about.

While it is important to train your mind to think of things that are creative, productive, and positive, it is also important to learn to stay insulated from the negative thoughts of others. Here is a very simple experiment in this regard.

Please don't think of a white elephant.

What did you just think of?

A white elephant. Right?

This is how susceptible our mind is to the power of suggestion. Imagine a group of students who have their class X board exams. They are standing outside the examination center, doing the last minute preparations, waiting for the door of the center to open. They are all going through their notes when one of their classmates arrives and starts telling nervously about how he is sure that he will not remember anything as soon as he looks at the paper. He keeps talking about how difficult the subject is and how unpredictable the examination papers have been in the past. Within minutes you will see that you too have started feeling a little nervous. While you were calm and relaxed a while back, you have now started panicking a little. Can you guess which state is better when you are about to appear for an important exam? Yes, calm and relaxed of course. So it would have been better if you had insulated yourself against the thoughts of the nervous student.

Swami Vivekanand has said:

"We are what our thoughts have made us, so take care about what we think. Words are secondary. Thoughts live, they travel far… Fill the brain with high thoughts, highest ideals place them day and night before you and out of that will come great work."

Gautam Buddha, the king turned ascetic on basis of whose thoughts Buddhism was founded, has said:

"All that we are is the result of what we have thought. If a man speaks or acts with an evil thought, pain follows him. If a man speaks or acts with a pure thought, happiness follows him, like a shadow that never leaves him… The mind is everything. What you think you become."

It is but natural that we face different kinds of problems – at work, at home, in personal life, in married life, in business, in career, even with our children and neighbors – the list is endless. Problems are part of our life. With the life getting increasingly complex, our problems are simultaneously on the rise. Despite the modern facilities and luxuries, we are a deeply unsatisfied lot. Our piece of mind is lost in the race for more and more. In spite of a lot of problems we are too busy to sit and think about the solution to these problems. We spend most of our lives solving day-to-day problems and have no time to train our minds to look at the bright side of things. Consider the following example of a professor and his students.

The Professor and his Students

One day a professor entered his classroom and asked his students to prepare for an important surprise test. The students all waited anxiously at their desks for the test to begin. They were all in their class XII and were preparing for their lives ahead. All of them were painfully aware of the fact that their performance in this year may decide their future. Needless to say, they were all under major stress.

The professor handed out the test paper with the questions facing down. Once he had handed out papers to all the students, he asked the everyone to look at the questions.

To everyone's surprise, there were no questions — instead there was a drawing of a terrible monster prowling a jungle. The professor, seeing the expressions on everyone's faces, said to them, "I want you to write about what you see on this paper."

The students, though still confused about the relevance of this test to their syllabus, got started with the task. At the end of the class, the professor took all the exam papers and started reading each one aloud, in front of all students.

All of them with no exception had defined the monster — its fangs, its red eyes, its lion-like mane, the blood dripping out of his mouth, and how it made them feel.

After all had been read, the professor started to explain, "I am not going to grade you on this. I just wanted to give you something to think about. All of you talked about the monster. No one talked about the jungle – the beautiful tall trees, the butterflies and bees, the birds sitting in the trees, the greenery – and the same happens in our life.

This was one smart professor indeed!

We know how stressful life has become for our younger generation right from the time when they are kids. But instead of helping them destress, we often add to their worries and fears. Life gives us the entire scene – the monster as well as the jungle. But we choose to focus on the monster and not on the beautiful jungle. We always have reasons to celebrate the gifts of life. We have our family, our loving children, our parents, we have a good job, a number of friends, and so many other joyful events happen in our life, but we tend to think about what went wrong, what is not so good etc. When in reality, the monster is much smaller than the jungle. We must learn to look beyond it. It is just a part of the larger picture. By forgetting this, we do ourselves grievous harm.

When we dwell too much on our negative thoughts, we surround ourselves with negativity, not only in terms of thoughts and feelings, but also in terms of actions. This state of mind does not take us too far. We don't feel happy no matter how well we do. We do not feel secure and confident. On the contrary, we become defensive, confrontational, self-centered, and cynical. Therefore, we need to look beyond our limited field of vision and work towards sowing, nurturing, and harvesting positive thoughts and actions.

Negativity can never yield anything positive. We waste precious time and energy in staying negative and the outcome of this state of mind is zero. We let go of opportunities, we ruin our relationships and we damage our professional lives by staying negative. While a positive person earns friends and well-wishers, a negative person merely attracts other negative people and, as a result, finds himself/herself much deeper in negativity. What goes around, comes around and so does negativity. So if you find yourself getting drowned in negativity, take action and help yourself. Banish the negative thoughts and think about what positive action you can take to pull you out of the situation.

It is easier to find faults with others than it is to make an effort to see the positive side of everything. Negative thinking has an immediate, destructive impact on our life. Negative thoughts distract us from our positive growth and from achieving our goals. This ends up making us feel even worse.

Remember that like attracts like. Positive people are drawn to positive energy and negative people are drawn to negative energy. A little introversion may help us avoid negativity. We should start to turn our thoughts away from negativity at the end of each day and guide our mind towards peace and benevolence. This enables us to carry greater and greater loads without feeling any type of burden. When our inner landscape is full of beautiful thoughts, everything we do will be a pleasure. It would calm down chaotic situations and offer solace to troubled minds.

No matter if you are a young person or old, whether you are a child or an adult, whether you are poor or wealthy, whether you are a teacher or a student. It doesn't matter who you are and what you do with your life. If you wish to achieve great things, you should know that you have it within you to make it happen. Every person on this earth has the ability to achieve greatness. Everyone has the ability to attain what he/she wants. It is possible for us but only when we know about the greatness of our thoughts. Creative thoughts require exclusive concentration.

When we think deliberately with full concentration about the goals that we want to achieve and train our mind to deal with distractions, we can come up with creative solutions to our problems. When we sieve out all other thoughts from our minds and concentrate on a single thought, it becomes very powerful and brings about our desired results.

But the irony is most of us do not have time to sit and think. While dealing with the normal chores of life, we allow things to happen as they come. Only in the case of any emergency or urgency we sit in a corner with a piece of paper and a pen in our hands and start thinking about what to do. But at such times, we are already so preoccupied that we only do what is absolutely required to be done, thus leaving no scope for creativity.

We must try to squeeze out time from our daily schedules to do some active, logical thinking. If it appears impossible, we should try to take time when we are taking bath, during morning walk, while eating breakfast, while waiting, or while traveling – and make it happen.

We mostly let our circumstances define the boundary of our existence. We feel that in order to live a life of abundance, we must be born into abundance and we feel that if we are living a meagre life, we must make do within it. This happens when we find our thoughts linked with our past that contained hundreds of limitations where there was no broader, brighter, greener, and free road to walk through. We try to pave a path like our father, forefathers, or elders had been doing, without looking into changed circumstances. In this way, we only tread over a narrow path and finally come to a dead end.

However, our past is not an example nor is it a guide to our current life or the future. It is just a bundle of events that happened. We must leave it at that, while extracting our lessons from it. If we have bright, evergreen and a vibrant outlook towards life today, we must look forward to living a brighter, greener, and more vibrantly abundant life tomorrow. Abundance is not about growing richer materially, it is about the value and wealth of our positive thoughts, our ability to think in the right way. Being big is not about becoming the richest man, biggest industrialist, or a famous leader. Being big is how we would like to be remembered by the world.

Consider this little story for example.

Alfred and the Wrong Obituary

About a hundred years ago, a man was reading a newspaper. To his surprise and horror, he found his name written in bold letters in the column of the obituary. The newspaper had reported the death of the wrong person by mistake. After getting over the initial shock, he carefully scanned through the obituary column where many people had posted their thoughts about him. He could not resist the temptation of finding out what people had said about him.

The first remark read, "Dynamite king dies."

Next remark read, "He was a merchant of Death."

This man was the inventor of dynamite and when he read the words "Merchant of Death" he asked himself a question, "Is this how I am going to be remembered?"

He got in touch with his thoughts, feelings, and decided that this was not the way he wanted to be remembered. From that day on, he started working towards peace. His name was Alfred Nobel and he is remembered today by the great Nobel Prize. Nobel Prize is named after this inventor of dynamite, who, through his constant, focused efforts, managed to change how the world perceived him.

Just like Alfred, we must think about how we would like to be remembered and decide over the quality of our thoughts that would pave a path of our future life.

Life can be framed within triple "E" – "Yesterday is Experience, Today is Experiment, and Tomorrow is Expectation." Let us use our experience in our experiments and achieve our expectations.

Albert Einstein once said:

"Try not becoming a man of success, but rather try to become a man of Value."

We cannot change the direction of the wind, but we can always adjust the sails to reach our destination. Our thoughts must concentrate on the journey we wish to take today. Instead of fighting the prevailing winds, we must adjust our sails to take us in the direction we need to go.

Watch Your Attitude

Our attitude is the product of both positive and negative emotions and energies. Being positive means having a positive attitude. An attitude is a forceful tool in our hands that can cause both success and failure. All around us, we hear judgments about others floating around – he has an inflated ego, she has a quick temper, he is sincere, she is hard working, he is a man of principles, she is honest, and so on. We usually do not stop and think about why a person is tagged in a certain way. Reputation develops over time. When you demonstrate a particular attitude for some time, it slowly becomes your identity. Just like everyone else, we too would have some labels attached to us. Our attitude defines our image in society. People dealing with us tend to work with us as per our image.

If our image is that of an honest person, they would put more faith in us. On the contrary, if our image is negative, they will always be on their guards. Therefore, it is important to build and protect your image with care.

Scholars have broadly categorized attitude into two types: positive attitude and negative attitude. In order to understand these categories, let us consider the following two examples.

This first one is common but very relevant.

Example 1 – Once a teacher walked into a classroom. She put an empty glass on her desk and from her water bottle poured some water into it. She then asked her students what they see when they look at the glass.

Some answered that the glass is half full.

The others said that the glass is half empty.

Students who saw the glass as half full were termed as optimists, or those who managed to see something good in all scenarios. Students who saw the glass as half empty were termed as pessimists, or someone who managed to see the dark side in all situations. Though this categorization may not necessarily be fair based entirely on how they perceived a glass of water, but you do get the drift.

Example 2 – Two salespersons went to a tribal area to investigate the market potential for garments. Both of them saw that nobody wore any elaborate clothes or garments there. They were all mostly scantily clothed and some wore no clothes at all. Both salespersons made their notes and returned. They submitted their reports upon their return. Following is the summary of the reports submitted by both:

First Salesperson: There is no potential here – nobody wears garments.

Second Salesperson: There is massive potential here – nobody wears garments.

Please note how the exact same situation was interpreted in two very different ways by the two salespersons.

While the first salesperson has a negative approach towards the situation, the second salesman is very positive about it. He/she sees opportunity that the first one failed to notice.

These are not the only examples. We encounter so many such situations in our day-to-day life. It is upon us how we interpret them. With a negative attitude, we can walk right past opportunities and not notice them. Whereas with a positive attitude we can find opportunities where none exist at least on the surface.

The salesperson with a positive attitude has a roadmap in his/her mind to tackle the situation; he/she is able to draw an action plan to act upon his/her observations (thoughts), whereas the first salesperson lacks this attitude. The salesperson with positive attitude is more creative. He/she is able to come up with new ideas about what can be done to encourage the tribes to start wearing garments, and what can be done so that business can be generated out of sale and purchase of garments. The second salesperson is able to see the glass as half full.

Human creativity and will power has the power to turn imagination into reality.

American author and motivational speaker, Jordan Belfort, has said:

"The only thing standing between you and your goal is the bullshit story you keep telling yourself as to why you can't achieve it."

The two examples cited above are an indication that what we make of our lives is related to how we perceive life. If we have a positive outlook and are willing to go through some pain to achieve what we want to achieve, nothing can stand in our way. However, we need to train ourselves to stay positive, to look for opportunity in every situation. We also need to shed our negativity as it can cost us some great opportunities.

In the words of Swami Vivekanand:

"It is our outlook that matters. It is our own mental attitude, which makes the world what it is for us. Our thoughts make things beautiful, our thoughts make things ugly. The whole world is in our own minds. We must learn to see things in the proper light."

In order to deal with negativity and to make our attitude positive, we need to make some deliberate efforts. How we wish to live our life depends upon us. What we wish to achieve during our lifetime, depends upon us. Nothing but our own negativity can prevent us from achieving what we really want to achieve.

LOOK AT THE BRIGHT SIDE

Life has its ups and downs. Everyone has some positive and some negative aspects in their lives. While it is difficult to completely ignore the negative aspects, it is important to focus on the bright side. This helps us choose positivity over negativity. This small tweak in what we choose to focus on can turn our entire life around.

There are many things in our life that we can't help. A family member is ill. There is financial crunch. Our career prospects do not look so great. Kids are not doing too well in academics. There can be number of things that aren't going too well with us. And some of these things are beyond our control. One thing that is in our control, however, is our attitude. And this is always true. No matter how many mistakes you have made, or how high or low you are feeling in life. If your attitude is positive, you can be happy and cheerful under any circumstance.

Consider the following example to understand this further.

The Trader and his Sons

There was once a small town and in this town lived a trader with his family. This trader had two sons. Once this trader incurred heavy losses in his business and ended up becoming bankrupt. The family started living in acute financial hardships. To avoid dealing with these problems, the trader started drinking and became an alcoholic. He became blind to the pitiable conditions of his family members.

The elder son saw his father's callous attitude and was very worried for the family. He started looking at what was left of their business. Soon he noticed that his father had been regularly visiting a remote village in order to procure material for his trade. He travelled to this remote village

*and traced down the villagers from whom his father used
to procure material. He spoke to these villagers and found
out that they had stopped supplying the material because
his father had been irregular in making payments. He
probed deeper and soon found out that his father had
been delaying payments because the agent dealing with his
father had cheated him of considerable money. The elder
son now went in search of the agent, and soon found him.
He first tried to convince the agent to make the payments,
but when the agent tried to act smart, the trader's son
threatened him with police and legal action. The scared
agent agreed to settle all accounts within a period of six
months. This was how the trader's elder son responded to
his father's state.*

*Let us now compare this to how the younger son
responded. When the younger son saw his father becoming
an alcoholic, he was so distressed that he also started drinking. Under the influence of alcohol, he often got in trouble
with the neighbors. Whenever he fell short of money, he
would steal from some place or the other. One day, the
police caught him red handed and put him behind bars.*

You can see how two brothers living in the same house,
going to the same school, getting equal treatment from their
parents, and suffering the same hardships were quite different
in their attitude. The elder brother was brave and responsible. He was positive and believed that if he took action, it
would yield some result. He was able to look at the bright side
of adverse circumstances and was able to find out a solution
to the problem faced by his family. What one can say about

the second son is that he was deeply impacted by his father's state. Some would even say that he was probably more sensitive than the first son, because of the way his father's condition impacted him. However, it is also true that he gave up at the first hint of trouble and followed in the footsteps of his father, bringing more misery upon his family.

Ask yourself this question – if you were to hire one of these men for a job, who would you trust? The elder son or the younger son? Our guess is that your response would be the elder son. We may sympathize with the younger son, but would probably have more faith in the elder son that he will be able to find a way out of any tough situation.

Our ex-President, late Dr. APJ Abdul Kalam has put this beautifully:

"All Birds find shelter during rain. But Eagle avoids rain by flying above the Clouds. Problems are common, but attitude makes the difference!"

Though the problems that will arise may not be in our control, it is always up to us whether we want to look at the dark cloud or the silver lining. We feel happy or sad, we smile or frown, we may dance or we may cry. How we react to a particular situation is all because of our attitude. And our attitude has a huge impact on our body language. If you develop a habit of thinking positive and giving your best to every situation, your confidence goes up. And when your body language exudes this confidence even under stress, your peers, seniors, family members, and friends, all place their trust in you. On the other hand, if you always look stressed and keep whining about your problems, you come across as someone who cannot handle tough situations gracefully.

But how can we go about making our attitude positive? It isn't as hard as it sounds. There are some subtle changes that you can make in your outlook and your surroundings that can make a huge difference. Try doing the following for a few days and see if you notice any difference in yourself:

1. Keep your workplace clean – this helps in staying organized. And once that happens, your thoughts automatically become clearer and focused.

2. Pay attention to your personal grooming. Look smart and dress well. You will feel much more confident.

3. Smile when dealing with people. This will help you make friends and you will notice that you are able to achieve more out of your interactions with people.

4. Make your language positive. Don't dilly-dally. Say it as it is. Honesty really is the best policy. For example, if someone working for you makes a mistake, tell them exactly what went wrong, but don't make it personal. Even if you are pointing out someone's mistakes, be objective. Talk to them about what can be done now to overcome the situation. What could have been done to avoid the situation can be discussed later once the crisis is over and the person who had committed the error is less stressed. Similarly, when you make a mistake and someone confronts you about it, don't be defensive. Take responsibility and figure out what can be done to emerge out of the situation

and also communicate what steps you are taking to avoid such mistakes in future.

THINK AHEAD

In today's fast-paced world, one needs to stay one step ahead of every situation. In other words, one needs to be proactive. Being proactive means to plan and align things in advance by foreseeing future risks, problems, and challenges. Some of us do draw our strategies by visualizing the future and organize things in advance to avoid any possible setback. Some of us do not visualize the future course of things and deal with situations as and when they arise. As a result, many of us do not have any control over the course our life is going to take. We like to call it "going with the flow". Going with the flow at times is the right thing to do, but why we do it that matters. If it is because we are too lazy or naïve to think and plan, then it is probably just that – being lazy. However, if it is a strategic move, then it may prove to be a smart one. One example of going with the flow as a good strategic move can be if we are looking for growth professionally, but we realize that the market is down and it is risky to switch jobs in such a scenario. We decide to persist in the current job for some time and wait for the right time.

The following example will further make it clear what beings proactive means.

Businessman and Two Clerks

There was a once a rich and successful business man who dealt in food grains. He used to purchase food grains in

large quantities from farmers and stocked them in his storage house. He was the biggest supplier of food grains to all retail dealers of his area. He was a benevolent person and used to take good care of his staff members. This included the two clerks he had appointed to keep the accounts and records of his business. Both the clerks had started working simultaneously five years ago, at the salary of Rs. 5000/- per month each. During the course of five years, the salary of the first clerk was increased from 5000/- to Rs. 50,000/- whereas the second clerk's salary had only been increased to Rs. 10,000/- per month.

Due to the large variation in their salaries, the second clerk always remained disheartened, depressed, and dissatisfied. One day he gathered the courage and asked his employer the reason for this partiality. "We are both working at the same post for the same number of years, then why is there such a stark difference in our compensations?" he asked. The businessman looked at him and smiled. In a calm and kind voice, he said, "There is no partiality, I am paying both of you according to the work you both are doing." However, the second clerk wasn't satisfied by this answer.

One day, a farmer arrived in the town to sell his product but stood a little far from the office of the businessman. The businessman saw the farmer and asked his second clerk to go and find out about the product he had come to sell. In order to prove his worth, the second clerk immediately went to collect the information and came back within a few minutes. He informed that the farmer was selling "rice". The businessman asked the second clerk further questions – which brand of rice he was selling, at what rate, and from where had he come. The clerk could not reply to any of the questions. He had not tried to find out because he had not been asked to do so. He had only been asked to find out about the product that was being sold and he had done just that.

Now the businessman sent his first clerk, who was drawing a salary of Rs. 50,000/- per month to find out the product that the farmer was selling. The first clerk too went away but did not return immediately. "He was taking too much time to complete such a simple task. Surely now the boss will realize who deserves better," thought the second clerk. He started daydreaming, making big plans about what he would do with the enhanced salary.

After a period of two hours the first clerk came back and informed that the product is rice grown in an area which is famous for rice. "It is good quality rice and the rates at which the farmer is selling it is also very competitive. Last month, Jag Mohan ji, one of our biggest customers, had sent us a demand for this very rice. He is willing to purchase this rice from us in large quantities. I have, therefore, offered to the farmer that we are willing to buy his entire lot provided he sells it to us at further discounted rates, and the farmer has agreed. I have advised our store keeper to arrange for the space to store this lot and therefore got delayed."

All this information was narrated in the presence of the second clerk, and the second clerk was now clear about why he was getting less salary compared to his proactive colleague.

Any prudent person who had been working in the field for five years would have done all of this. Not only had the first clerk found out about the product, but he had also ascertained its quality, rate, and found out prospective buyer to avoid future losses and storage rentals.

It is very easy to criticize others and that is why we often come across people who are ready to criticize us and our work. Unknowingly, we too could be doing this to the others. There can be no better example than that of Indian cricket team. Almost all Indians are "experts" in cricket and at the drop of a hat offer suggestion on how the captain should have sent a more aggressive batsman at this juncture, or how the bowler should have bowled a Yorker, or how the batsman should have played a sweep shot. God forbid, if our cricket team loses a match, we immediately term them as failures. We criticize the captain, the players, and the selectors. However, we do not realize that they are the experts in their fields and we are just armchair critics. Had we been in their situation, we would probably not have been able to do as much as they had done.

This is true in our lives as well. People who have no experience in our fields and people who do not know what it is like to be in our position are ready to judge us and appraise our performance. They are happy to offer suggestions on how we can do a better job. There's nothing wrong in offering help and suggestions, but when done in a patronizing way, can be very irritating. But often we invite this kind of behavior. Consider the following example.

The Painter and his Painting

Once upon a time, a very famous painter made a beautiful painting of the King. He wanted to gift it to the King on his birthday. In order to ensure perfection in his art, he displayed a copy of the painting on the crossing of the main market. This area was visited by a large number of people every day. The painter put a label on the painting requesting everyone to point out the mistakes in the painting. He kept a box of pins next to the painting and he intended people to use these pins to point out the mistakes.

Next day when he went to see the response to his painting, he was shocked to see that the entire painting was covered with pins. It seemed that everyone who had been there had managed to find a fault with the painting. He was very disheartened to see the number of mistakes he had made. "Had I gifted the painting to the King as it is, the king would probably have fired me or even sentenced me to death," the painter thought.

He discussed this with a friend and the friend started laughing. When the painter asked why he was laughing, his friend said, "You will find out soon enough. Just do what I ask you to. Put the painting at the same place. Just change the note this time."

The painter placed another copy of his painting at the same place along with a note, which read, "Please rectify my mistakes, if any. Please put a pin at the place where you make the correction so that I may learn from your expertise." Beneath the painting he also put all colors and paintbrushes.

The next day the painter went to see what kind of inputs he had received this time and he was surprised to see that not one change had been made to the painting, not one pin had been stuck on it. The paints and the brushes were lying untouched. Confused, he went to speak to his friend again and the friend told him, "It is easy to criticize just for the sake of it. However, when it comes to adding real value, very few people are capable of that. The people who had pointed out your mistakes earlier can't even achieve what you have achieved. And that is why when it came to actually doing some work, they shied away."

Nobody is born perfect. All of us have faults but most people are in the habit of finding fault with others. Instead of obsessing about what others think about us, we should be convinced of how well we have done our job. We must be satisfied with our own work and should know within that we have given our best. This is the only way to develop confidence on ourselves.

ACCEPT POSITIVE CRITICISM

However, critics are not always wrong. It is important to identify constructive criticism. We must prepare ourselves to consider criticism that is constructive and that helps us to improve ourselves and the way we do our work.

American entrepreneur and motivational speaker Jim Rohn says:

"Don't spend most of your time on the voices that don't count. Tune out the shallow voices so that you will have more time to tune in the valuable ones."

So how do we identify valuable, constructive voices from a sea of noise? This is a very important skill to learn. Constructive criticism points out our mistakes and shows us where and how improvements can be made. We should, therefore, consider constructive criticism as a useful feedback. We should take it as an opportunity to learn and improve. These voices indeed help us become better. When we develop the ability to identify constructive criticism and the ability to listen to negative comments without losing temper or confidence, it means we have become discerning and sensible.

DON'T UNDERESTIMATE OTHERS

We meet hundreds of people during the course of our business, work, and career and in connection with other fields of life. The first look of the person, the style of their clothes, the way they talk, the way they speak leaves an impression on us. We obviously need time to understand people, especially the ones we do not know at all, but many times we form our opinions based on the outward appearance and his/her demeanor in a particular moment. And because of this we make the mistake of underestimating or overestimating someone's abilities just on the basis of our first impression of them. The following example will highlight how quick we are to form opinions about the others and how inaccurate these opinions can be.

A Villager and the Bank Manager

A tired looking villager wearing very simple clothes with a turban on his head and old, unpolished slippers on his feet approached a bank Manager and requested him to open his bank account. By his looks and his clothes, bank manager thought him to be a poor man who wished to open a bank account for his future savings. "To open a bank account, one has to deposit some money with the bank," the Bank manager told him. "How much money do you want to deposit?" asked Bank manager. The villager replied, "One." The manager thought the villager wanted to deposit Re. 1 only for opening the account. As per the bank's guidelines, the minimum deposit was at least Rs. 1000 to open an account. So the bank manager explained, "It is not enough and you are required to deposit a bigger amount if you want to open an account." The simple villager said, "Okay. But I have travelled a great distance. Can I have a glass of water?" "Sure!" the bank manager said and ordered someone to fetch water. In the meanwhile, the villager pulled out a simple mobile phone from his pocket, dialed a number and started talking to someone, "Beta, you have the wrong information. One cannot open an account with Rs. 1 Lakh. We would need more. I will ask the manager how much and maybe we can visit the town again next month to open the account."

The bank manager was stunned. He had obviously formed a wrong impression of this simple villager. He quickly apologized to the villager and started the proceedings for opening the account.

This is how we too behave in most situations. If we are interviewers, we tend to be in awe of candidates who are well-dressed, can speak well, and at times do not really try to drill deeper. We assume that a candidate with this much confidence must be good. On the other hand, if a candidate is simple and nervous, we tend to infer that the person is probably not as qualified as the candidate who is well-dressed and confident. But our judgement may not be accurate. In the long run, the person who appeared confident may turn out to be overconfident and unwilling to learn, whereas the person who appeared nervous may turn out to be sincere and patient. So we need to hold back on our judgement for a while and try to dig deeper in order to find substance.

Let us flip this situation around. Just like we are quick to judge everyone, everyone else too is quick to judge us. Our first impression can make or break our career.

When we first meet someone not known to us, he/she forms a mental image of us instantly. People will make dozens of assumptions about us within seconds. Based on our attire, appearance, posture, and facial expressions, they would form opinion about our education, experience, success, and our knowledge. We are painfully aware of this fact and most of us try our best to present ourselves in the best possible light when meeting someone important for the first time. However, what is the longevity of this first impression? This depends upon the situation. If it is someone who is required to judge you based on a short interaction, an interviewer for example, the first impression will indeed be very important. On the other hand, if it is someone with whom you are required to work for a few months, you can work towards building a reputation slowly.

People say, "the first impression is the last impression". We have heard this maxim several times in our life and we use it as a "Golden Rule" for judging people. After all, individuals have several facades of their personality. Which layer of his/her personality carries his inborn instinct is always difficult to judge in a short span of time. It takes some time to understand the nature of any individual. Some people, by nature, are not made to push up real layers of their true self and are difficult to judge by their first appearance or impression. They do not intentionally hide any aspect of their character by virtue of their style of living and are often misunderstood by others. In the first instance they may appear rough, arrogant, harsh and egoist, whereas their true value remains beneath the surface.

On the other hand, some people pretend to be someone they're not, and try to impress others by adopting a style of impressive personalities. Their true identity remains buried under the layer of a self-created artificial impression. Such people are more careful about their first impression.

And, therefore, it is important not to treat the first impression as the last one.

We do meet people who look very charming, polite, soft-spoken, and humble. We take no time in categorizing such people as "nice". We get swayed with their charismatic personality without really waiting to find out more. There is a hint of magic or a spell that the charming person throws over us, sometimes simply in order to manipulate us and to control us. They may use charm to get us to do what they wish us to do. This charm may impress people with wisdom, intelligence, and virtues too. Some of the most famous conmen, the ones that get featured in newspapers, are people with charming personality and the ones that have a way with the words. We do not mean to say that every charming person is out there to take advantage of us. We just want to emphasizes that someone's charm should not be the only factor based on which you form a negative or positive judgement about the person, especially if you have just met this person. You should wait and watch and time will tell.

WE ARE NOT ALWAYS RIGHT

Our opinion of the world and the people around us is the ultimate truth to us. Each of us normally tries to look at life from our own single point of view and assume that what we think is right. We base our actions on our opinion. We do not stop and consider that we may indeed be wrong. However, this can be a costly mistake.

We lose out so much if we do not consider other's points of view. In fact, this lack of consideration may lead to disagreements, quarrels, and disharmony which may create a number of problems for us. It may be easy for us to get wrapped up in our own views believing that what we see, what we feel, what we think, and how we react is always correct. Even in one single situation, each person involved may have different opinions and points of view.

Consider this example for instance.

Two Students and a Teacher
Nikhil and Sahil were in their secondary school and got into a heated argument about some situation. Nikhil was

convinced that he was right and Sahil was wrong. Sahil was sure that he was right and Nikhil was wrong. Both were adamant and were not ready to consider the other's point of view. Seeing their argument take an ugly turn, the teacher intervened. Knowing about the matter of the argument, the teacher decided to teach them a very important lesson.

He brought them up to the front of the class and asked Nikhil to stand on one side of his desk and sent Sahil to the other side. In the middle of the desk, he placed a large, spherical object. He asked Nikhil, "What is the color of this sphere?" Nikhil could clearly see that it was black. He vehemently said, "It's black". The teacher then asked the same question to Sahil standing on the opposite side of the desk. Sahil, without wasting much time, said, "It is obviously white."

Nikhil claimed that he was right and Sahil insisted that he was right. Both boys were confused, but none of them was ready to consider the point of view of the other. This led to another argument about the color of the object. Now the teacher again intervened and interchanged the locations of the boys. Nikhil was now asked to stand where Sahil was standing and Sahil was sent to take Nikhil's place. Both the boys were again asked the same question. Nikhil was amazed to find that the object was "white" and Sahil was stunned to see that the object was "black". In reality, one side of the sphere was white and the other was black. The boys only had to exchange their places to understand the other's perspective of the sphere.

The story tells us that sometimes we need to look at a problem from the other person's perspective too in order to fully understand a situation. In the above situation, both boys were right in their respective perspective, but were blind to the other person's perspective. Arguments happen because there are multiple perspectives to any situation and each perspective is right on its own. When these multiple perspective combine, the situation becomes complete. Consider the example of a housewife bargaining with a vegetable vendor. As per her, the vendor is selling tomatoes at a very high rate. As per the vendor, he is selling them at a discounted price. Let us examine both their perspectives. The housewife is comparing the price of the tomatoes to the price at the *mandi*, whereas the street vendors is adding his cost of transporting these tomatoes and is also looking at making some profit. Both of them are right. They just need to understand each other's perspective and then may be a fair price can be worked out.

Once a man asked Swami Vivekanand, "what is the reason for every misunderstanding?" Swami Vivekanand replied, "The reason is, we see the people as we are, but not as they are."

Considering others' point of view gives us empathy and an ability to resolve conflicts in an amicable manner. It helps us win friends. As a leader, empathy helps us inspire people and bring out the best in them. People love, trust, and confide in people who have empathy. If you wish to be truly successful and to stay successful, you need to value empathy and inculcate it.

10

Keep Your Communication Clear

If we were to represent the activities we do in our lives in a pie chart, communication will probably be one of the largest slices. Most of the activities we do, in fact, involve communication in some form or the other. Think about it. Even when we are watching television or listening to music, we are involved in some form of communication, where we are receiving someone's thoughts. At home, in office, during our leisure time, we are never really isolated from the world. And nowadays even when we are alone, doing nothing, we almost always have a smartphone in our hands and we are sharing statuses on Facebook, or chatting with our friends. An activity that occupies such a large chunk of our lives cannot and should not be taken lightly. Communication should be done very responsibly.

At times the fate of relationships, or someone's job, may depend upon the way you communicate.

At times we hear our national leaders make some very embarrassing comments for which they are later forced to tender apologies or issue statements like "I was quoted out of context." One simple way to avoid such situations is to think before you speak.

Greek Philosopher Plato said:

> *"Wise men speak because they have something to say;*
> *Fools because they have to say something."*

Communication is an essential and a very important part of our life. All our relations whether personal or business depend upon it. Communication is a very important ability that all living beings are blessed with. It is ultimately upon us how effectively we use it. We can choose to use this ability constructively with words of encouragement or destructively using words of despair. Most of the problems in our personal or professional relationships occur due to ineffective communication. The purpose of communication is to express our thoughts, our heartfelt feelings, and our mind. We communicate to express our needs, requirements, desires, and thoughts. We communicate to ask questions and learn about the world around us and to engage with others. Communication is not confined to words alone, it can mean our facial expressions, our body language, our presence and even our absences and silence.

At any given time, we communicate with people around us and with ourselves. And most of the times we don't even realize it.

Communication has occupied a place of importance for ages and will continue to do so because of its vital function of conveying one's feeling to another. Explicit communication may be oral, typed, or handwritten. Whatever be the case, the basic principle of communication is that others should understand what is being communicated. If not, the purpose of communication is defeated.

Poet William Butler Yeats said:

> *"Think like a wise man but communicate in the language of the people."*

The problem arises when our words or our language of communication is ambiguous and conveys a meaning that may impact our listeners adversely or may mislead them. Sometimes we don't mean what we say and sometimes we do not say what we mean.

A single thing can be said in many different ways. One way can bring fruitful results and the other way may cost us heavily. What is the reason that when two people make a similar request one is welcomed and the other meets a strong resistance? It all depends on who we speak to, what is our body language, what is our facial expression and what is our relationship with the other person. The response we receive depends upon how we communicate.

Our words are under our control only until we speak them. Once spoken, these words have a life of their own and are free to be interpreted in any possible way by the one who hears them. So it is better to be careful.

When we were kids, our teachers taught us a lot. Some of them had a natural way with children, while others had to resort to punishments to get their points across. Some teachers had the power to show us the way forward, while others had this ability to drag us down, to make us lose our confidence. With some teachers, we could open up, discuss our issues and problems, while others made us shiver simply by looking at us. When we think about it, it all boils down to communication, be it verbal or non-verbal. When we are in a position where we can influence young minds, we need to remember how other people made us feel with their words and gestures.

Apart from our words, our problems also stem from how we speak them. Our gentleness, harshness, volume, speed, everything means something and can have different effect on different people. Our words and our tone work together to create an impression of us in the minds of our listeners. Consider this example for instance.

Shivam and his Boss

Shivam reports to Nandita. Their team has successfully delivered a project and has worked really hard for the last couple of months. He desperately need to take a leave. However, it is still too soon after the delivery and from his past experience he knows that the client often faces several issues during the first few days and may require some hand holding. Getting leaves approved in such a situation is tough, and moreover he has already had some issues with Nandita, who believes that he hasn't behaved very responsibly during the release. He nevertheless decides to try his luck.

Shivam is almost sure that his application will be rejected. He enters Nandita's cabin and in a low voice says, "Boss, now that the project is over, I was planning to take a few days off? Is it okay by you?" Nandita looks at Shivam and asks, "how many days and when?" "Starting tomorrow," he replies, "may be a week."

"Tomorrow?" asks Nandita. "And you are telling me now?"

"Well, if I had known earlier, I would have told you earlier. Wouldn't I?" Shivam couldn't help the sarcasm. Despite all the work I have done for this release, she doesn't trust me, he thought.

"So this is unplanned leave. And you need six days off? SIX DAYS?" asks Nandita, her temper rising. She was already irritated with Shivam. "Do you understand the implication? Who will deal with the client queries? You are the most experienced member of the team, I expected better planning from you."

"I have managed this entire project so well, and you still doubt my planning? I was just asking you. If you don't want to approve it, fine! I will not take an off," he said angrily, and stormed out.

Especially when we are carrying some past baggage with a person, communication becomes even more challenging. In this situation, Nandita is approaching the communication with a belief that Shivam is not responsible, and Shivam is approaching it with a belief that Nandita doesn't trust him. Both of them needed to be extremely careful with what they say to each other and how they say it. May be if Nandita hadn't assumed that Shivam had already planned his vacation and was deliberately informing her late, she would have phrased her question differently. "Tomorrow? Could you postpone it for a couple of days so that we can plan how things will be handled in your absence? In general, if you are planning a longish leave, it's better to give a few days' notice." would have been a better question by far. It would have conveyed her concern that Shivam needed to plan his vacation better and also opened up a route for negotiation. On his part, Shivam should probably have started off with showing that he cared about his responsibilities and had planned for them to be handled. "I am sorry this is a little sudden, but I am feeling quite stressed out. If it is okay, can I take a few days off? I realize that we are expecting some queries from the client, but I can brief Neha and she can help take care of them till I come back. I will anyways be available on phone and email." This would have worked better. This would have shown that Shivam realizes that his request is going to cause inconvenience and he is ready to support the organization even during his vacation if need be. The conversation would have been completely different then. Moreover, Shivam's storming off at the end again does not send the right message. It is a passive aggressive approach and will never get you anything. If there is something to discuss, stand your ground and discuss it.

Many of our problems are created due to our ineffective communication. We not only have to be polite, positive but also creative while communicating with all our expressions and gestures working together with a smile.

Emma Thompson, a much-loved British Actress said:

*"Any problem, big or small, always seems to start with
bad communication."*

BE A GOOD LISTENER

Successful communication involves at least two parties – the
one who speaks/writes/sings/performs and the one who listens/
reacts. It is safe to say that listening is also a very important
aspect of communication.

Words may play a game with us. Right words can often be
interpreted in a wrong way. During the course of the conversation, we usually remain stuck to ideas with which we are
deeply involved. In this state of mind, our interpretation is
biased. The first and foremost rule of good listening is that
you should try to keep your biases at bay when you are listening to someone. Consider this example.

The CEO and his Employees

*The CEO of a company while visiting the workplace asks
a simple question to several of his employees separately.
The question was asked simply because of curiosity. The
question was "What are you doing?"*

Following are some of the responses that he received:

*Employee 1: "Sir, sorry! I am just going to start my
work immediately."*

*The employee obviously hadn't yet started his daily
work. Upon hearing the question, he/she assumed that
the CEO had noticed the same and that is why was asking*

this question. For the next few hours, he/she would probably keep thinking about this, though the CEO would forget all about it.

Employee 2: "Sir, Narayan requested me to help him complete his project. I was just going to start my work."

This employee is giving unnecessary justifications. He/she perhaps hopes to score some brownie points by stating that he/she is helping fellow workers. This too does not work because CEO is really just making polite talk, and would once again not remember this. Moreover, the CEO is also bound to see through the employee's blatant self-promotion.

Employee 3: "Sir, has something gone wrong? Am I not doing my work properly?"

This employee might have committed some mistake but hasn't yet confided in anyone. That is why he/she is being so clearly defensive.

Employee 4: "Sir, I am working on a most interesting presentation for a client. Would you like to take a look?"

This employee is clearly proud of the work he/she is doing and doesn't have any stories in his head. Enthusiastic and eager, this employee will probably stand out in the CEO's memory of the trip in a positive way. And the CEO may also agree to the employee's request of seeing the presentation. Simply by being unbiased, this employee has opened up a great opportunity of himself/herself.

Staying focused while listening to someone is more challenging than it seems. It is very common in meetings and speeches, but even when someone is sharing their soul with you,

you can embarrass yourself if you are a bad listener. You can in fact end up losing friends. Very often, while listening to the others, we are more concerned about what kind of image we are projecting. We don't realize this but this definitely comes in the way of how well we are able to comprehend what the other person is saying. So when you are listening to someone, focus only on listening.

A wise person has said: *"It's not easy to listen to something, even if it's good advice. We are set in our ways, we know what we know, and we think how we think. It is hard to listen, harder to change. But when we do open our hearts to some good words of advice from those before us, we usually end up grateful for the new food for thought."*

Indeed, it is easier to become a good orator than a good listener. Listening is not only a vital communication skill but a great art of learning. To be a good listener requires absolute concentration of mind and heart. Mostly we are not at ease to listen to others as we tend to think and talk more about our own point of view. We must remember that listening is a very important skill in all aspects of our lives – from getting a new job done, learning new things, taking notes in class, preparing for some presentation, or even maintaining our personal relationships.

Mind that listening may be a matter of displeasure also. Something said by others may hurt our feelings. We must be prepared to listen to negative comments also because they are a source of feedback on our style of working and thinking. We must not lose our temper or confidence over negative comments.

Epictetus, the Greek philosopher wrote:

"We have two ears and one mouth – for a good reason. It's more important to listen than it is to talk most of the time."

FOCUSED COMMUNICATION

Unfortunately, many of the things that we assume should be easy to do are in fact very difficult. Staying focused on one topic during conversation is one of them. We watch many debates on the television, and can see how difficult it is even for professional moderators to maintain decorum and keep the discussion focused on a topic. The problem with this type of discourse is that nothing useful ever comes out of it. Same is the case when we are talking to our friends, or when we are having a meeting to resolve an issue in office. In order to make productive use of everyone's time and to take serious steps towards resolution, we must stay focused. One solution in case of meetings could be to appoint a moderator to drive it. This moderator can have just one focus – to ensure that each participant stays focused on the agenda.

BE AWARE OF THE POWER OF WORDS

Be careful of what you speak. A very well-known proverb equates words with the arrows being shot from a bow. Just like these arrows, our words too cannot be recalled. They will reach and impact the target irrespective of anything.

Words carry enormous weight, and, therefore, they do have long-lasting effect. Negative words, in particular, can have long-lasting results. Every word that we speak has a force that creates powerful effect, either negative or positive, depending upon how and for what the word has been used. We use words to communicate with each other, but are often unaware of their power that may create an imbalance in our life.

Spiritual teacher and bestselling author Don Miguel Ruiz, has put this perfectly:

"The word is not just a sound or a written symbol. The word is a force; it is the power you have to express and communicate, to think, and thereby to create the events in your life. You can speak. What other animal on the planet can speak? The word is the most powerful tool you have as a human; it is the tool of magic. But like a sword with two edges, your word can create the most beautiful dream, or your word can destroy everything around you… Depending upon how it is used, the word can set you free, or it can enslave you even more than you know."

To create happy and encouraging events we must resort to words that bring fruitful results in our lives.

Bruce Burton explains:

"For good or bad, our conversation is our advertisement. Every time we open our mouth we let others look into our mind."

While communicating with someone, there should be no place for arguments and it should have no link with the personal life of others. We must learn to use the best words in any conversation irrespective of the level of talks and the result thereof.

We generally feel the heat of wrong words used for us by other people. In place of facing hate, humiliation, insult we may perhaps prefer to bear the loss and scrape the very issue of discussion and decide never to communicate with people who have hurled derogatory words for us. We must therefore also feel such heat for others. We do not communicate to gain victory or to win a war, we communicate to create a wave of energy that helps us to create our events of life and the circumstances congenial for the purpose of communication.

Sometimes we hurt ourselves with our own words. In fact, we don't realize it but we are constantly doing it. When we tell ourselves things like "I am a failure" or "I am hopeless" or "I am good for nothing" or "I won't get well", these words carry a wave of the impact that adversely affects our life. They occupy a permanent place in our personality and we start feeling their impact in our practical life. Be sure to make a choice to say the best possible words to yourself. Words like "I can do it", "I have done this before", "I am beautiful", "I am good with people" can go a long way. Once we say these words to ourselves, they become real.

PRAISE GENEROUSLY WHEREVER IT IS DESERVED

Genuine, heartfelt praise has a power beyond regular speech, but we use this power rarely. Usually when we see someone doing a good job, we feel jealous and this jealousy stands in the way of our actually praising the person. We are happier to stay silent then, but are quick to find faults with people at every opportunity. However, praising someone can be therapeutic. Try it some time. Next time your colleague, your competitor, does a good job, praise him without any resentment. See how that makes you feel. It makes the other person happy too, but you too feel good about yourself. You feel like a good person. When dealing with our juniors, we must use praise as an act of wisdom to raise someone's hopes and aspirations so that they can work towards creating a more congenial atmosphere around themselves. It works on the principle that when you give something, you get it back with interest.

However, we must be careful to praise only when it is well deserved, else it becomes flattery.

In the words of American poet William Arthur Ward:

"Blessed is he who has learned to admire but not envy, to follow but not imitate, to praise but not flatter, and to lead but not manipulate."

THE POWER OF SILENCE

There are many ways by which human beings communicate. We talk, we write, we sing, we emote, we use gestures, and we also use our silence. Probably more than we realize. Silence, in fact, is a very powerful mode of communication. We are the most powerful when we are silent. In most vulnerable conditions of acute negativity, keeping silent can be the most effective and impressive way of communication. It provides us inner strength to experience trust and self-worth. It is from this base of inner strength that our actions evolve. Silence can achieve a lot when used strategically.

Following are some common examples when we use silence:

1. To Convey Our Disagreement

"You have the right to remain silent…" you may have heard this sentence in many crime shows. This sentence is a part of the standard Miranda warning that is read out to any suspect before he/she is arrested. Contrary to popular belief, silence doesn't only signify acceptance. It also signifies that you disagree. When a manager makes an announcement and the entire team is cheering. If one person is standing in the corner silently with a wry smile playing on his/her lips, this silence rings louder than all the cheers, and is often viewed as silent disagreement. The person may not be happy with the management's decision.

2. To Convey Our Acceptance

This is an idea widely propagated by Bollywood. In an oft-repeated scene in old Bollywood movies, we often see the heroine run inside when a proposal for her marriage is being discussed. This act is often seen as agreement to the proposal. If to a room full of people someone says, "Do you see some problem with the proposal?" and the audience remains silent, it is understood as our having accepted the proposal.

3. To Communicate that We don't Know

Simply because someone has asked us something, unless it is during a one-on-one interaction, we do not need to respond.

Many times, by providing wrong answers to a question, we make our ignorance public. If a question is not directed to us alone and we do not know the answer, we can avoid sounding like a fool by staying silent.

4. To Convey Our Displeasure

This happens most often in personal relationships. When we are cross with someone, we remain silent. This is especially relevant to couples. When one person is unnaturally silent for some time, the other should guess that the person is angry. It is time then to introspect and see what we could have done, or not done, that could have made our partner angry.

5. To Maintain Peace

At times it is best to stay silent. Especially during heated exchanges, if one party chooses to remain silent, the angry discourse doesn't survive for too long. American writer and journalist, Ambrose Bierce has said:

> *"Speak when you are angry and you will make the best speech you will ever regret."*

As humans, we are programmed to respond when asked a question, or even otherwise. However, silence used at the right moment is the best communication strategy. It prevents a lot of heartache.

Benjamin Franklin has rightly said:

"Remember not only to say the right thing in the right place but far more difficult still, to leave unsaid the wrong thing at the tempting moment."

CONFIDENT AND POSITIVE COMMUNICATION

There are so many variables in a simple email being sent from one employee to the other. And each variable impacts how the communication is being conveyed and received. Our personality, our past, our experiences all reflect in the way we communicate with one another. Our choice of words, our tone, our body language ensures that each communication isn't just about the topic being discussed. All forms of communication are multi-layered. Apart from what is being discussed, each bit of communication also subtly sends out information about us and our personality, about our relationships with other people, and about our opinions on various things.

Any recipient of a communication is free to interpret our words differently, based on their own life experiences, their impression of us, their understanding of the issue being discussed, and their own personality. It isn't possible to discuss communication without discussing these variables. Let us, therefore, discuss them one by one.

1. Impact of Our Personality and Experiences

We have been communicating all our lives, right from the time when we were born (may be even before that to our mothers by communicating our food cravings and by reacting to voices we liked) till today. And we will keep communicating in some form or the other throughout our life.

While a baby communicates by smiling and crying, a toddler communicates by using simple words or sentences or a variety of gestures. After that, as we keep getting older, the way we communicate keeps changing. By this, we do not mean only in terms of words and grammar, but also in terms of the words we choose to use or how we frame our sentences. For example, a timid person is likely to use a lower volume than a gregarious person. Someone who is confident is likely to use different words when compared to someone who lacks confidence. Consider the following examples:

Statement 1: "Umm… in my opinion we should do tell the contractor to go ahead."

Statement 2: "I may be wrong but maybe we should ask the contractor to go ahead."

Statement 3: "I think we should ask the contractor to go ahead. What do you think?"

Statement 4: "Please ask the contractor to go ahead."

If we analyze each of these statements individually, we realize that they are all spoken in the same context. However, the personalities of the speakers are different. In case of statement 1, we see some hesitation on the part of the speaker. This shows us that may be the speaker isn't entirely sure that this is the best course of action. The speaker also uses the phrase "in my opinion", which subtly acknowledges that others may have a different opinion. This statement also indicates to the listener that perhaps other people too should be consulted before a final decision is made.

In case of statement 2, the speaker starts with a negative phrase "I may be wrong... This tells the recipient that he/she must first assess whether the speaker is indeed right. Basically, the recipient cannot take any decision based on this statement alone. This kind of language probably will not work well if used by someone who is a decision maker; on whose judgement his/her subordinates or peers rely. A decision maker needs to be sure and accountable. He/she needs to take tough and risky calls at times and if he/she cannot do it with confidence, then there can be a big question mark on his/her suitability for the post.

In statement 3, once again it seems that the speaker isn't sure about his/her decision. Moreover, the speaker wants the recipient to share accountability for the decision.

Statement 4 is conclusive. It leaves no doubt in the mind of the recipient. This is the language of someone who is confident, has authority, and is willing to be held accountable for his/her decision. The communication is authoritative and yet respectful. This sounds like someone who is used to being in a position of power.

2. Impact of Our Relationship with Others

At times, we let the nature and quality of our relationship with the recipient or other stakeholders impact the way we communicate. For example, the way we communicate with our seniors is markedly different from the way we communicate with our peers or our juniors. And the way we communicate with people we trust or have good relationships with, can be different from the way we communicate with people we do not trust or do not have a cordial relationship with. While it is natural for some of our biases to creep into our regular interactions, when it comes to professional relationships, we need to be very careful.

Consider the following statements, for example:

Statement 1: "Check with your team and let me know how this issue got missed."

Statement 2: "Please could you check with your team and let me know how they missed this issue. I would also like to know your thoughts on how this type of a miss can be avoided in future."

Statement 3: "This is most worrying. Please check with your team and let me know how this issue could have been missed. Did they even look at its functionality?"

Statement 4: "I am sure you are already looking into this, but could you please update me as soon as you have identified how this issue was missed? Also share your thoughts on how we can avoid this going forward."

Statement 1 is direct and without any baggage or any preconceived notion. One can detect a level of authority in this statement and this was probably spoken by someone higher up the corporate ladder to someone much junior. The lack of "please" makes this a command instead of a request.

Statement 2 was probably spoken to a peer or may be to someone one level junior. However, there is a hint of respect. The speaker is polite and in general respectful to the others. However, if need be, the speaker can pose tough questions and demand answers without really offending the other person.

Statement 3 is steeped with lack of trust. The speaker assumes that it is possible that the recipient's team has probably not looked at its functionality at all. If these words were spoken by someone who has been in this position for long and has been interacting with the same set of people, this statement indicates that there have been similar incidents in the past that have made the speaker doubt the capability of the team in question. On the other hand, if these words were spoken by someone new in the team, it indicates that the speaker is quick to jump to conclusions and probably needs to be a little tactful.

Statement 4 indicates that the speaker has been working with the recipient for long and there is some level of trust between both the parties. The speaker is concerned about the issue being missed but at the same level trusts the recipient's ability to handle this. The speaker obviously cares for his/her relationship with the recipient and values it enough to maintain respect even during times of conflict.

3. Impact of Our Opinions

Our opinions – political, personal, philosophical, societal – all become a part of our language without our realizing as much. These opinions, especially political, personal, and societal, may not come up in professional communication, but are mostly apparent in the discussions we have with our friends or in any other group. People can guess our political inclinations by the way we react – verbally or otherwise – to the opinions of the other people. While in day-to-day life, this does not matter as much, if we let our opinions cloud our judgement and come in the way of our work, they can cause our career serious harm.

Consider, for example, a manager who thinks that a woman can't be trusted with responsibilities that require her to stay late at times or work from home. Such a manager can create hindrances in the career growth of the female members of his team. He can end up frustrating them. Though in the short run, this manager will cause harm to the career of other people, in the long run, his prejudices may come in the way of him reaching his full potential.

4. Impact of the Recipient's Personality

We all know that communication is two ways. While a lot depends upon the person who is conveying something, the way the recipient receives it also matters. In fact, at times the meaning of what is being said changes completely while being passed from person to person. The popular game Chinese whisper is a very basic example of this. A piece of information when passed from recipient to recipient often changes form completely by the time it reaches the person it is intended to reach. While in the game this deterioration mostly happens because of ineffective listening, in real life there are many other sieves that cause the information to change when it is transmitted from one person to the other. We have already discussed how this happens at the speaker's end. Let us now discuss how the recipient's personality may impact communication.

Consider the following example:

Statement: "May be you should seek help on this task," says the boss.

Employees may interpret this differently based on their own personalities and past experiences. One employee may interpret this as the boss's proactive thinking and concern for the project. A second employee may interpret this as the boss's lack of trust on him/her. It all depends upon the recipient's own level of confidence and basic personality – a cynic will always find reasons to doubt the intention, an optimist will always find something good in the email, someone who is too touchy may find the tone sarcastic and so on. In order to really understand what someone is trying to say, at times it is important to avoid reading between the lines. It is often safest to just go by the words in the communication and not try to think too much about the tone in which it was said.

5. Impact of the Recipient's Relationship with the Speaker

The same thing may sound different to you depending upon from where it is coming. If it is coming from a professional rival, a simple request may sound sarcastic to you. If it is coming from someone who hasn't demonstrated faith in your work, a simple request to confirm something may appear as if the person has questioned your integrity. It is important to learn to identify such interpretations and put them aside, before you react to the communication.

You can see that the variables that may impact the quality of communication between two people may end up clouding our judgement. Therefore, when you are sending or receiving communication in any form, make sure you put aside all these biases and look at it from a neutral point of view. You will be surprised at how easy communication becomes when you are able to do this.

Be Mindful

Over the past couple of decades, we have seen the human civilization change at an unprecedented pace. In the 1980s, analog telephones (remember the huge, black instrument with a dial?) were just becoming regular household things. Computers had just been introduced as a subject in school, and Internet was all but non-existent. Life was simpler in many ways. Back then, most of us whose parents held day jobs, were used to spending time with them once they were back from office. They did not bring their work home, and we did not have various communication devices to keep us busy. We were more present to what we were doing at the moment and to people who were around us.

But as technology evolved and Internet happened, our day-to-day lives were swamped with devices of all shapes and sizes. And these devices made the world smaller, brought our friends closer to us, made information available with the click of a button, or the tap of a finger. The transformation was nothing short of magical. Next came Social Media and various other ways to keep ourselves engaged in the virtual world. Now, the warm family scene transformed. They are still sitting together after work, but each with a Smartphone in their hands. At work we have multiple tabs open on our browser window and we are always online on Facebook, Twitter, Instagram etc. You name it, and we are there. We are everywhere except in the present place and time. So no wonder a trait like mindfulness needs to be reclaimed. We need to remind ourselves about our responsibility in the present moment. A way of being, which was ingrained is us, now needs to be practiced and learned.

The following definition of mindfulness probably conveys exactly what the trait means when applied to worldly, day-to-day lives of individuals:

> *"Mindfulness captures a quality of consciousness that is characterized by clarity and vividness of current experience and functioning and thus stands in contrast to the mindless, less 'awake' states of habitual or automatic functioning that may be chronic for many individuals."*
>
> **—Brown & Ryan**

Let us first understand "mindlessness". Stating it simply, when you are distracted and aren't paying your full attention to the task at hand, you are being mindless. Following are some situations to consider:

➠ Anurag is sitting at home watching his favorite show on the TV. Alongside he is also chatting on WhatsApp with his friends. In the process, he keeps missing some important scenes in the show that he is watching, so he plans to watch the rerun during the night.

➠ Vinita is having her breakfast and is also engrossed in an interesting book. At the end of the breakfast, she realizes that she has eaten too much.

➠ Sagar is working on a report that he needs to submit in an hour. The report requires complex calculations and data mining. On the side, he also has Facebook open on his browser and keeps scrolling through his timeline. Half-an-hour later he realizes that he had got some of the initial figures wrong and he needs to redo most of the calculations.

➠ Anjali has had a terrible day at work. Once she is back home, she is packing gifts for Diwali. But her mind is still at work. After some time, she realizes that she has no idea which gift she has packed in which gift-wrap and whether she has struck out the price on all. She has to open all the packets again and check.

None of the individuals above are really paying attention to anything they are doing. They may be under the impression that they are handling multiple tasks at the same time, but in reality, they are not doing justice to anything they are doing. Anurag isn't paying attention to the show he is watching. He will now end up spending another hour late at night watching the same show. By not being mindful when she is eating, Vinita is headed towards multiple health issues. Sagar is in serious risk of missing his deadline. Anjali's preoccupation with what happened at office has also impacted her time at home. All this wasted time and energy could easily have been saved had these individuals been mindful. Mindlessness brings productivity down. Mindlessness takes away the value you can get from any activity.

With the dawn of information technology, the term "multi-tasking" has become very popular. Scientists have worked hard to device multi-tasking algorithms to make computers work faster. And we have started using this term in context of human activities too. Along with our machines, we too are expected to evolve at the same rate. However, if you really dive deep into this concept, multi-tasking is nothing but scheduling. At the end of the day, most machines, if you go to the core of their functioning, are only scheduling and prioritizing. At an instance of time, they are only involved in one task. They may switch between tasks at a very rapid state, but that is really all they are doing. To expect human brains to focus on two things at the same time is, in this case, ridiculous. Human multitasking is a myth. With the exception of intuitive tasks such as breathing, walking, blinking etc, your brain cannot focus on two activities at the same time.

As more and more people are realizing this and are also taking note of the amount of stress "multi-tasking" causes, the word "mindfulness" is gaining popularity. It is being perceived almost as a new concept. We have forgotten how mindful we used to be by default when there weren't so many distractions to deal with.

Being mindful isn't too difficult but it may need practice. It is simply about being present to your task, your surroundings, and the people around you at any instance. If you are in a meeting, mindfulness is about being alert to what is being said. This may sound easy, but if you have held a corporate job, you would know how easy it is let your mind drift. And then before you realize it, you have missed an important point. When you are participating in a sports tournament, mindfulness is about being present to the game. Being alert to the positions and signals of your team members. Being alert to the positions and moves of the opponents. When you are in a conversation, mindfulness is about being alert to what everyone else is saying. It is also about being present to silences and expressions. Only when you are really there, taking each moment as it comes, can you be mindful.

At this point, you are probably already thinking how different the world would be if everyone was mindful. Indeed, there are many benefits of staying mindful. Let us now talk about some of them.

1. IMPROVED PRODUCTIVITY

When you are distracted, you may take twice as long to finish a task. Moreover, the quality of the work you do will also be questionable. Let us consider the example of two colleagues Rajesh and Sunaina. Both work in the same team and both are at the same position. Their department is expecting some visits by the client and their boss wants to give a presentation to the client about the work his team has been doing. He also wants to use this opportunity to showcase what else his team can do. His intention is to get more business for his organization. As the time is short he asks Rajesh and Sunaina to help him on a few of slides. After briefing both of them on what he expects, he divides the work equally amongst them and asks them to start working. While Sunaina was mindful during the discussion, Rajesh was distracted. His son needed to be picked up from the school and he needed to organize that. So instead of paying attention when the boss was giving the brief, he was planning this in his mind.

Now when it came to preparing the slides, he based his research on what he thought was the brief. And even while preparing the slides he was preoccupied. As a result, he got delayed in preparing the slides and, to top it all, the slides he prepared were based on inaccurate brief and the quality of his work was low. When Rajesh and Sunaina presented their work to their boss, the boss immediately saw that while Sunaina's slides only required a little tweaking, Rajesh's slides required major rework. He was disappointed in Rajesh' work and because of shortage of time, he asked Sunaina to quickly redo what he had asked Rajesh to do earlier.

Though on the surface there weren't any major repercussions of this, his boss lost trust in Rajesh and when the client gave their organization more work and someone needed to be promoted to manage that, Sunaina was obviously considered more suitable for the position. With this example, you can probably see how being mindful during the conversation and work benefitted Sunaina. You can also see how being distracted actually cost Rajesh a promotion. A simple solution to this would have been for Rajesh to focus on the briefing and later take 5 minutes to plan the pick-up of his child.

2. REDUCED ANXIETY LEVELS

All of us have heard that meditation helps us relax. Many of us have tried to meditate but given up on it when we were not able to achieve the thoughtless state that one is supposed to strive to achieve during meditation. Let us try to understand what this state of thoughtlessness is. In traditional meditation, this state is achieved when we are able to focus on a point and banish all other thoughts from our mind. However, this requires a lot of practice to achieve. For most of us, as soon as we try to banish thoughts from our mind, more thoughts come flooding in. Now let us consider a situation where we are focusing on completing one task. At that instance in time, we are being mindful. Our thoughts are limited to that one task. We are focused. Isn't this similar to meditation? If you think about it, any kind of work, when done with focus can be equivalent to meditation. When you practice being mindful, when you are present to here and now, you are reaping the benefits of a session of meditation. And as a result, you are much more relaxed at the end of it.

There's another way to look at this too. If you have done your work with focus and in a mindful state, you are mostly confident that you have given your best to it. And when you reach this state in your work, your anxiety levels go down, and you are no longer fearful.

3. IMPROVED CONFIDENCE AND SELF-RESPECT

When you believe in the quality of your work and this belief doesn't waver for a prolonged period, your confidence automatically goes up. This reflects in how you walk, how you talk, in your entire personality and it is quite visible to everyone else too. Your body language changes, your image in the organization changes, and more important than all this, you do not wait for other people to acknowledge you are good. Your sense of worth stems from your own confidence in your abilities. And this is really the best state to be in. You become the kind of person who can be entrusted with responsibilities. You become the person everyone else looks up to. If you are mindful in your conversations, you will likely have great relationships with your colleagues. World starts changing around you, and you are the root cause. If this isn't reason enough to try to be mindful, then what is?

4. IMPROVED PHYSICAL HEALTH

Mental health is directly proportional to physical health. A person who is focused, confident, happy inside, is more likely to take care of his/her body. Such a person is less likely to develop stress related illnesses, such as hypertension and heart problems. This type of a person is more likely to want to live a long and happy life and as a result really work towards staying healthy. Therefore, you will see that a person who practices being mindful in all situations, is more likely to be healthy physically as well.

There are many more benefits of mindfulness, like clarity of thoughts, clarity of communication, increased self-awareness, and improved social life. If all this has made you think about mindfulness, go ahead and try it. You will be surprised at the transformation you will see in yourself.

Surviving Bad Days

Each day is different and some will probably not be as good as the others. What should be done then? Stay hopeful. Hope keeps us going. You are still the same person who once became successful solely because of your capabilities. Not because of luck or fluke, but because of your own skills and talents. You still have those skills and talents, and this failure is just another experience in life. It will teach you many things. Be ready to learn from them.

You have recognized yourself and found your values; you know your goals and vision for life. This failure is simply a temporary setback. Life, by no means, is easy. It is difficult. Every day we face many problems, many obstacles, and we have to work with all impediments and barriers that obstruct us.

We have to make sure we keep moving towards our goals, in spite of the difficulties we face. If we remain hopeful, we can find strength within to conquer all barricades and to draw a specific strategy to overcome our failure and plan to be successful in achieving our goals.

Michelle Obama has said:

"You may not always have a comfortable life and you will not always be able to solve all of the world's problems at once but don't ever underestimate the importance you can have because history has shown us that courage can be contagious and hope can take on a life of its own."

If in crisis, you can stay hopeful, you can get over any loss, any failure and you can be an inspiration for others.

Consider this little story for example:

Shiv and the Bicycle

Shiv was a school student. His school was far from his home, which was located in a remote village. Every day, Shiv had to walk for hours to reach his school. Shiv wanted a bicycle on which he could ride to his school. The problem was that his father was a poor farmer who could not afford to buy his son a bicycle, but, unwilling to break his son's heart, he kept promising that he would buy Shiv a bicycle as soon as he was able to save some money. A very long time passed, and Shiv's father was still not able to save enough money. Every day Shiv hoped to get his own bicycle but it was all in vain.

One day while returning from his school, Shiv fell in a drain and broke his spine. He was seriously injured and was admitted to a government hospital. The doctors and other medical staff provided the best of treatments available but his condition remained serious. The staff was seriously worried about the young boy.

All this while, Shiv's class teacher was getting worried in the school. Shiv was a good child, brilliant at studies and all his teachers liked him very much. Upon contacting Shiv's family, the class teacher learnt of Shiv's accident and went to the hospital to meet the boy. She was shocked to see Shiv's condition. His entire body was bandaged, legs were stretched out, tied with rope to the ends of the bed. Shiv was obviously in acute physical pain. The class teacher remained with Shiv for some time, talked to him, and in the end returned from hospital without talking to anyone else.

After about a week when the class teacher again visited the hospital, a nurse asked her, "What did you tell that boy? Ever since you visited, his attitude towards recovery has improved." The teacher was surprised and listened carefully as the nurse explained that the entire staff had been worried about the youth. He had not been responding positively to any treatment, nor had he been showing much improvement. "But ever since you visited, Shiv became more responsive to treatment. It appears now that he wishes to get better as soon as possible," the nurse explained.

The teacher hadn't performed any miracle, but had simply promised Shiv that he would have a bicycle as soon as he recovers and is fit enough to ride it. After the teacher's *visit, everything had changed for Shiv and he started on his path to recovery. He was still in pain, his body was still bandaged all over, and he wasn't yet able to walk, but even in this darkness, he began to experience the light of hope. He envisioned himself riding a smart new bicycle to school every day and saw himself peddling furiously to get to school in time. Though his own father had promised him the bicycle many times, Shiv had been disheartened because the promises had never been fulfilled. And as he had grown up, he had realized that he would never really have that bicycle because his father was struggling to make end meets at home. He had given up. But with the teacher's promise, the hope had been rekindled. The hope triggered happy visions of future, and that, in turn, triggered recovery.*

Hope gives strength to fight the odds of life. People with hope have the will and the necessary inclination to achieve goals. Hope gives positivity. Hope creates an environment conducive to positive outcomes.

Hope is not just a feel-good emotion; it is a driving force that leads us to our goals that are conducive to growth and improvement. No matter what life crisis we may face, we must always think positively, hope for the best, work for the best, and act for the best. We must recall the troubles and trials we have experienced and overcame in the past. We might have survived destructive relationships, gone through a hard professional crisis, battled a major illness, or experienced a period of grief. In one way or the other we had tapped into hope during that time, just know that we can do it again.

When our days seem bleak, it is hope that keeps us going from one day to the other. When the night seems too long, it is our hope of seeing the dawn break that makes it possible for us to sail through the night. Hope has the power to heal. It has the power to turn failure into success. It has the power to help you overcome the most difficult of hurdles. Hope has the power to help a weak army overthrow a strong enemy. It is hope that makes our life worthwhile.

Have you ever said to yourself "I hope I will be selected for this job," "I hope my project will be completed in time," "I hope my company will make profit this year." Simply by hoping for these things, you are creating a possibility for things to happen. And once the possibility is created, you need to follow it up with action and attitude to make it happen.

Hymn writer Isaac Watts has said:

"Hope thinks nothing is difficult; despair tells us that difficulty is insurmountable."

All hopes may not be fulfilled, but never give up. Because some hopes are fulfilled and you should put in your best to ensure that you yourself are not the reason why your hope is not fulfilled. Don't worry about the factors beyond your control. You cannot do anything about them anyway.

The reason most people never achieve their dreams is because they simply give up. Life isn't meant to be easy; we will need to fight extreme lows but will also get to enjoy extreme highs.

The times when we are feeling low test our determination, and we need to stay hopeful to emerge victorious.

Story of Ira Singhal – Topper of UPSC Exam 2014

If you have the will, nothing can ever stand in your way. Ira Singhal proved this. Ira suffers from scoliosis, a spine-related disorder that hampers her arm movement. She made history by becoming the first physically challenged woman to top the UPSC exam in the general category. She is currently posted in the Indian Revenue service. She has broken all barriers and proved that nothing can stop us from achieving what we really want to achieve, if we truly believe in our dreams. Strong will power and confidence can take you where you want to go. She is one bold girl who refused to give up on her goals. She made the entire system bend before her will.

When she topped the UPSC exam in 2014, it was her fourth attempt. She had cleared the exam in 2010. At that time, she was denied a posting because of her disability. She took the matter to the court and while the court was considering the case, she chose to keep appearing for the exam to improve her rank. She topped in 2014 and also won the court case. She is now posted as an Assistant Collector.

Beating all odds of life, she proved that disability is only a state of mind. If you have the willpower, anything is achievable.

Talking about being denied a posting earlier, Ira said in one of her interviews with the Indian Express, "it was a big disappointment, a major setback then. But I decided to fight back. It was tough initially as I had to undergo tests, submit medical certificates and prove that I am capable of doing jobs entrusted to me in the IRS. For two years, it was tough but then everyone realized that I am capable of working in spite of the disabilities. They realized I am no pushover."

Inspiring, isn't it? Like Ira, we should demonstrate infinite energy, infinite zeal, infinite courage and infinite patience, and only then can great things be achieved.

HOPE MUST NOT BE BLIND

Staying hopeful does not mean that we should close our eyes and accept that everything we hope for will be achieved. Achieving what you hope to achieve requires overcoming many challenges, and we must be prepared to accept these if we really want to achieve what we hope to achieve. Hope drives our energies to push us closer to our goals but beyond that it needs passion and hard work.

American writer Rebecca Solnit says:

"Blind hope faces a blank wall waiting for a door in it to open. Doors might be nearby, but blind hope keeps you from locating them."

The door to success may be at an arm's reach, but we cannot just sit and hope that someone will come and open it for us. We have to put in our efforts and use our strength, intellect, and other resources to open the door. We must not waste our time on flimsy hope backed by no wisdom. Such blind hope becomes our weakness instead of strength.

Abhay and Astrology

Abhay suddenly incurred heavy losses in his business. He put in all his efforts to revive it, but the business continued to sink lower and lower. One day, he discussed this state of things with his friend Sanjay, who advised him to see an astrologer about this and seek help. He even recommended a great astrologer who had supposedly helped Sanjay's family many times. This instilled some hope in Abhay and he too contacted the same astrologer.

The astrologer studied Abhay's charts for several minutes and then did some calculations. At the end of this ceremony, he announced that Abhay was in the grip of dubious planetary movements and this was affecting his luck adversely. In order to turn the planetary movements in his favour, Abhay was advised to arrange for a grand ceremony to appease God and the stars and planets by performing a yagya. The astrologer also asked Abhay to be generous to Brahmins and donate huge amount of money to the priests who would conduct the yagya.

Now, Abhay was very hopeful. This sounded like a simple enough solution. He started making all the arrangements to conclude the ceremony. He not only spent huge amount of money in organizing the ceremony, he also donated huge sum to the local temple and to the two priests performing the ceremony.

In this exercise, he not only spent valuable time but also atrocious amount of money. However, his business continued to plummet.

Worshipping God and offering prayers may provide us a sense of solace and peace of mind but hoping that it would somehow make things happen for you magically is foolishness. Besides hoping for positive things to happen, one also needs to take active steps towards solving the problems.

Therefore, it is important to distinguish between hope and blind hope. Hope is a sign of optimism that helps us sense and strive towards a bright future. On the other hand, blind hope is just wishful thinking. Unless followed by action, it exists only in our imagination.

FACING FAILURE

Many of us, despite having crossed difficult hurdles and faced tough challenges, continue to live in the fear that we may sometimes fail to achieve our objectives. We worry that we will fail to deliver and will, therefore, be exposed as fakes or as someone who in the past succeeded by fluke. We are quick to discount how much hard work we put in to get to this stage. We do not give ourselves credit for our successes and, therefore, keep on living in insecurity.

While it is true that we often live in false insecurity, it is equally true that we may fail to deliver at times. It may be because of some external factors beyond your control, it may be because someone else failed to do their job, and it may also be because you made a mistake. Many of us are defensive about this. Many of us shy away from accepting that we messed up, that we were careless, or that we made an uninformed decision. We worry that if we accept our mistake, people will stop trusting us.

However, we fail to realize that by being defensive or by trying to find and give reasons for our failure or by pointing fingers at the others, we come across as someone who is afraid of taking responsibility for his/her action or choices. And this, in the long run, can truly damage our career. However, on the other hand, if you are seen as someone who owns up to his/her mistakes and is responsible enough to think in terms of how to get past the situation and to make sure that this does not happen again, your colleague's respect for you will increase manifolds.

We are human beings, and we are bound to make mistakes. Everyone does. How we deal with the mistakes we have committed matters. Consider the following scenario for example:

Zareen and her Attitude

Zareen was a hard-working software engineer who had been working in a multinational for several years. She was a very talented developer and was up for promotion shortly. In order to judge her capabilities and also to hone her abilities as a manager, she had been made an informal team lead for two of her juniors – Akanksha and Junaid.

Zareen was a soft-spoken person who was able to make people comfortable very easily. With time both of her team members had started trusting her. They followed her instructions and respected her opinion. She would often allocate various types of tasks to both of them and then guide them through these tasks if and when they got stuck.

There was one such assignment that was allocated to her team. This assignment was critical to the organization and was, therefore, being monitored by the senior management. The assignment involved the team capturing some critical organization data in the real-time and raising alarms when it crossed a certain threshold.

Zareen allocated the task to develop this solution to Akanksha, who started working enthusiastically. However, she soon ran into a problem where the technology she was using was preventing her from capturing the required data. She did some research and identified some alternate technologies that would allow them to proceed.

Zareen looked at the list, praised Akanksha for her proactive research and asked her to use the technology that seemed to be the easiest to implement. Akanksha went ahead and did just that. Very soon the application was up and running and was ready to be demoed to higher management.

During the demo, everyone was impressed by the results. Very soon they were all discussing the underlying technology. Zareen happily told them about how her team had found a way around the regularly used technology. When asked to share about the alternate technology that was used, Zareen proudly shared the name. One of the senior directors was familiar with the technology and asked Zareen whether they had ensured that the security hole had been plugged. Apparently, the solution that Zareen's team had used had been diagnosed with a serious security hole that could potentially allow hackers into an organization's network. Zareen did not know about this. Needless to say, the higher management was concerned. At this point, Zareen could have responded in two ways:

Response 1: Zareen could have accepted that her team member had probably not done a good enough research. She could have promised to have this checked and in case the solution was indeed found to have security holes, she would herself take over the development work and complete the task with high quality.

Response 2: Zareen could have appreciated the input by the senior director and promised to have it checked. She could have admitted that she should have done this in the first place. She could have promised that she would get security testing done for the entire application to ensure that no other security hole had crept in.

Which of the responses do you think you would have respected more if you had been among the senior management? Our guess is Response 2.

Response 1 indicates that though Zareen is okay with taking the credit for the success of the application that her team had developed, she was not ready to take the responsibility if it failed. Response 1 also indicates that Zareen's team cannot trust her and even the senior management needs to be careful while trusting her with an important assignment.

On the other hand, Response 2 indicates that though Zareen may make mistakes, she is open to constructive feedback and can be held accountable for her decisions. This also means that her team is in safe hands and the senior management can trust Zareen with critical assignments.

Zareen opted for Response 2. The senior management agreed that this should have been checked earlier, but they were happy that the possible problem had been acknowledged and Zareen was going to take suitable actions to correct/prevent it. On the whole, they were happy with the way the job had been done and gave a great feedback to Zareen's seniors. Zareen was promoted that year and the two people who were earlier informally reporting to her now became her formal reportees, along with several other folks. She had already gained a reputation of being a fair, responsible manager and her team was very happy to be working with her.

BUT WHAT IF IT IS A HUGE FAILURE?

Things ultimately worked out for Zareen. However, there may be situations when you act in a responsible way and accept your mistake, and yet you suffer the consequences. Your mistake was perhaps too grave to overlook. The organization had to take an action against you. In other words, yes, you failed and you failed catastrophically. What do you do now? You will probably feel very low. You may want to hide in your home and not face anyone. You may lose trust in yourself.

The first step is to acknowledge your emotions and to tell yourself that it is okay to feel this way. Then, if you find that you are not able to cope, you seek help from your family and friends – in other words, your ecosystem, which we will discuss in the next chapter. You may feel hesitant to approach them at first, to mingle, to respond to their well-meaning enquiries such as "how are you?" If this too does not help, seek professional help. Visit a psychologist or a counselor. In other words, keep making efforts. Don't let yourself fade away. Everyone makes mistakes. You did too. You failed, but that does not mean that you cannot bounce back. Things will get better. They always do. This too will be behind you very soon. And you, yourself, can accelerate the process.

We take our failures as our weakness but can we imagine a life that is full of joys and no sorrows? Can we think of sky without clouds, a day without night, and sea without waves? When we think about ourselves we always think of success, we don't think about our failures even in our dreams. We must know that life cannot always be a bed of roses. Difficulties are an inevitable part of our life.

Swami Vivekanand has said:

"In a day when you don't come across any problems – you can be sure that you are traveling in a wrong path."

We are bound to face some failures and many difficulties in every field of our life but we must not be bogged down by them. If we let them affect us in such a way, we lose sight of our destination. Problems and difficulties should not be able to stop us. They are indeed a good opportunity to strengthen us and help us progress with more experience and enthusiasm. We must keep moving forward, leaving the obstacle behind.

Bhagavad Gita is the perfect text to quote from here, for this was the crux of this great book:

> *"You have control over doing your respective duty, but no control or claim over the result. Fear of failure, from being emotionally attached to the fruit of work, is the greatest impediment to success because it robs efficiency by constantly disturbing the equanimity of mind."*

We already know that things are never going to work out exactly the way we expect them to, and if we keep on learning from our failures, we shall become wiser and keep moving towards our desired destination.

Winston Churchill said:

> *"Success consists of going from failure to failure without loss of enthusiasm."*

No doubt we cannot control our all situations but we can definitely control our attitude to fit those situations. We should not be disheartened by our failures, and instead should try to overcome them.

Philip Catshill and his Circumstances

Philip Catshill, a former British Police Officer, is now an independent author, artist, and poet who lives in London. His journey has been quite remarkable. And if he, in his circumstances, can overcome his disadvantages, then anyone can. At the age of 30, this young police officer suffered a head injury followed by a stroke. However, he didn't give up and after a struggle of 18 months, joined his job again. But his troubles were far from over. 11 years later, his wife left him and he lost his home and his family. But he refused to give up and once again found someone to love. He was welcomed into this new family, but this happiness too did not last. Just 16 days after his second marriage, he was in a road accident and suffered his second stroke. Now he was forced to give up his work. However, he wasn't the one to give up. He took refuge in music and art. He learnt how to play piano and tried his hand on painting. In the year 2011, as he approached his 60th birthday, he decided to write about his experience after his first stroke. And since then, he hasn't looked back. He is still writing.

"My first venture into becoming an author was nearly my last, but one characteristic I share with the fictional protagonist in my crime novels is we do not give up. We never say, 'I can't.,'" says Catshill. "I'm on a mission to prove to the world that despite being a 60+ wheelchair-using person with a three times stroke-damaged brain and a heart problem, I am perhaps less-abled, but certainly not disabled! I can still achieve success in everything to which I set my mind, whether that's learning to play piano or continuing to play the violin with only one working hand, studying for and obtaining a university degree, painting pictures which have been described as breathtaking, or writing books which have so far reached the final rounds for two international awards. I am trying my best to inspire others towards success but not by saying, 'if I can do it, what stops you?' but I encourage with support, help, advice, and guidance wherever my limited abilities allow."

Casthill is now devoted to writing and provides help to thousands of his followers. A sign board out of his office reads:

> *"I am here with time to spare*
> *Which I give freely to*
> *Support, help, advice or guide*
> *Fellow writers and artists*
> *Whenever and wherever I can."*

We will see many successes and failures throughout our life. Some of them will be because of external factors, but others may be of our own making. Whatever be the reason for the failure, learning from it and trying to overcome it leads to humility, flexibility, and resilience.

American Author Og Mandino has said:

"Failure will never overtake me if my determination to succeed is strong enough."

LET OUR FAILURES BE OUR STEPPING STONES

All of us have gone through periods when everything seems to be going against us. If we are an engineer, a doctor, a clerk, a businessman, or in any other profession, at any given point in time we can reach a turning point in life where everything seems to be going wrong. It can be our project proposal that has been rejected, our product which has been slammed by the customers, or our decision that might have gone horribly wrong. But we are not alone. We can take comfort in the fact that many famous and successful people have known defeat, suffering, struggle, and loss, and have found their way out of the depths. These people have an appreciation, sensitivity, and an understanding of life that fills them with compassion, gentleness, and a deep loving concern.

SUCCESSFUL PEOPLE DO NOT JUST HAPPEN

We are not a failure just because we failed. However, we are certainly failures if we give up on our dreams simply because we have faced a failure. Let us look into the history of successful people who reached the heights of glory; all of them struggled a lot and overcame unbelievable hurdles to become successful.

1. Abraham Lincoln

The 16th President of United states, Abraham Lincoln, didn't have it too easy. His first romantic interest, Ann Rutledge, died at the age of 22. His first business venture did not take off. He married Mary Todd in 1842. The couple had four sons; three of them died before attaining adulthood. Today he is often ranked as the best US President of all times. The reason simply is that he did not let any of his failures/misfortunes stand in the way of his work.

Here's what he thought about failure: *"My great concern is not whether you have failed but whether you are content with your failure."*

2. Albert Einstein

The German-born theoretical physicist and Nobel Prize winner Albert Einstein didn't have it easy either. He faced many challenges in his life. His theories and writings were opposed by many anti-Semitic Germans and Europeans. He lost his professorship in Nazi Germany. This could have meant end of the road for some, but not for Einstein. He blew those assumptions away and became not just a great scientist, but one of the greatest scientists to have ever lived.

Here are his thoughts on failure: *"You never fail until you stop trying."*

3. Amitabh Bachchan

Amitabh Bachchan is now known as one of the greatest cine stars of Bollywood. He was at the peak of his career when he started his company Amitabh Bachchan Corporation Ltd (ABCL). This venture did not succeed and Bachchan was reduced to bankruptcy. However, the brave man refused to give up. He reinvented himself as the host of *Kaun Banega Crorepati* (KBC), and since then has never looked back.

4. Arunima Sinha

Arunima was a national level volleyball player. In the year 2011, she was thrown off a running train by robbers. She survived, but her leg had to be amputated. Less than two years later, in May 2013, Arunima surprised the world by becoming the first female amputee to climb Mount Everest.

She was awarded Padma Shri, the fourth highest civilian award, in the year 2015.

5. Eminem

15-times Grammy award winner Eminem has sold over 172 million albums worldwide. However, he has had his own share of personal problems. He dropped out of high school, had problems related to drug abuse and poverty, and depression, which led to an unsuccessful suicide attempt.

6. Henry Ford

Henry Ford, a billionaire, and founder of the famous Ford Motor Company, tried many automobile ventures that did not succeed. The first company he founded, Detroit Automobile Company, could not produce good quality automobiles at a reasonable price and was dissolved. The second company Henry Ford Company, in which Ford was the chief engineer, was renamed the Cadillac Automobile Company after Ford had to resign and leave. But Ford did not give up and today the company he founded in 1903, Ford Motor Company, still remains one of the biggest automobile companies in the world.

Here's what Henry Ford thinks of failure: *"Failure is simply the opportunity to begin again. This time more intelligently."*

7. Oprah Winfrey

Oprah Winfrey was born into poverty and was molested by her cousin, uncle, and a family friend when she was a teenager. When she was 14, she gave birth to a son who died in infancy. She was sent to live with her father and there she opted for a part-time job at a radio station. Very soon she became a popular radio jockey. She launched her own production company and became internationally syndicated. Her show *The Oprah Winfrey Show* became the highest rated television program of its kind in the history. She is considered as one of the most influential women in the world. She has also been ranked as the richest African-American of the 20th century.

8. Steve Jobs

Co-founder of Apple Inc. and Co-founder of Pixar Animation Studios, Steve Jobs was devastated and depressed after being sacked from the company he started, for his failure to make Mac a commercial success and for being too demanding a boss to his employees. However, he did not give up. Along with another colleague, Jobs launched another computer company, NeXT and also Pixar Animation Studios. However, as Apple started losing ground, they acquired NeXT and Jobs was back in Apple. The next year, Jobs became the CEO of Apple, but this time he made it a point not to repeat the mistakes he had made in his previous turn. He led Apple from success to success from then on till his death in 2011.

Here's what he thought about mistakes: *"Sometimes when you innovate, you make mistakes. It is best to admit them quickly, and get on with improving your other innovations."*

We can see how everyone, including those who seemed to have everything, suffered great pains during their lives. Fearing failures, if they had given up and never tried again, we wouldn't have ever heard of them. Similarly, we must not be disappointed if we fail in one attempt and keep on trying again.

Robert the Bruce, the King of Scotland, led a war against the King of England six times and was defeated all six times. He had lost all hope of victory and was forced to retreat. But he got up, tried for the seventh time with new vigour and won the war against his adversary. But here's a thought: What would have happened if he had refused to get up and had not tried for the seventh time? It's simple — today Scotland would not be recognized as an independent nation.

We most of us have a tendency to see, wish, and want a life that's easy, something as easy as a walk in a park. But the reality is indeed a bitter truth and the truth is that no one can be exempted from tasting failure in their life if one wants to achieve one's goals. Someone who has ever accomplished anything worthwhile has never done so without undergoing hardships and facing failures.

Nurture Your Ecosystem

"No man is an island" declared English Poet and Cleric John Donne. His philosophy was that the entire mankind is connected and if one man dies somewhere, whether you know about it or not, it somehow diminishes you. This is a very touching thought indeed. And if considered in the context of relationship, it is also true. Alone, we are nothing. If it wasn't for people we love, people we interact with, people we have any kind of contact with, we wouldn't have mattered. People are only relevant in context to each other.

Your family, your friends, your loved ones, your colleagues, your bank manager, your doctor, your investment consultant, your house help, the stranger you bump into on the street, the stranger you pass without noticing, all of these people define you. They are your ecosystem.

With the advancement of technology, most of us have started living in a cocoon. We usually stay detached from others even when we are having lunch with them. There are enough options available to keep us entertained without any interaction with an actual human being. Human interaction is in fact now a major distraction in our lives that revolve around a virtual world, which we access through our electronic devices.

Independence is important but it does not have to mean total disconnect from the rest of the world. We are human beings and, at the most basic level, need to feel a sense of belonging, acceptance, importance, security, and mutual respect. Even in the virtual world, we find ourselves surrounded by people who share their tiniest achievements in order to receive some "likes". This is how hungry we are for approval. It is sad that instead of depending upon our actual ecosystem for such emotional needs, we have started depending upon virtual acquaintances.

With time, this leads us towards loneliness and even depression. Social media cannot replace actual relationships. A strong, healthy relationship can be one of the best supports in our life. Good relationships help improve all aspects of our life, strengthening the mind, health, and our connection with the others.

Many of us, while working hard and fulfilling our familial responsibilities, forget to have fun. We forget how relaxing it can be just to have a conversation and share a meal with a friend. In fact, our society goes a step ahead. We are programmed to feel guilty if we are doing something just for fun, just for ourselves. We desperately need to get over this complex. Doing things for yourself is perfectly natural and as long as what is fun for you doesn't become nuisance for others, you should go ahead and enjoy. Spend quality time with friends, have heart-to-heart talks, play games, do things that relax you and make you happy.

It is a general observation that when our need for social relationship is not met, we fall apart mentally and even physically. It is, therefore, a must for us to create good and healthy relations with people of our choice, liking, and temperament.

There are moments in our life when we feel defeated and depressed. There are times when we feel that we will drown in our problems. Such moments drag us towards darkness where no ray of hope is visible. The outer world has no time or inclination to sit beside us, to console us, or to share our grievances. This is the time when our own relations, connections, friends, and relatives come forward to share our difficulties by sparing their time, money, efforts, and emotions. They not only provide us moral support but encourage us to fight against all odds of our life by boosting our lost energies. We must develop a network of deep relations with the members of our society. In the long run, the relationships we have developed, the people we have won over, and the goodwill we have collected are our most valuable assets.

To build a relationship we must have a great foundation of understanding. Without good understanding of relations, closeness will be restrained. Closeness is that aspect of a relationship that gives us a chance to interact freely and frankly.

Fulfillment in our social interactions can contribute towards leading a satisfying and successful life.

Even if some relations have turned sour, don't cut the cord because dirty water may not quench our thirst but it may still douse the fire. Even oldest and forgotten relations at times stand the test of time.

A Friend in Need

Two friends, Udit and Mudit, were studying in the same class in the same school. While Udit was an average student, Mudit was the star of the class. He topped the class in each exam and was ahead in sports and extracurricular activities. As a result, he was a favorite among the teachers too.

Whenever a difficult concept was taught in the class, all classmates would ask Mudit for help. Mudit, however, was moody and would help only if he felt like it or if he could extract a favor in return from the said classmate. Though he was at the top of the class, he was also very insecure. He would rarely help students who he thought could score better than him. Convinced that everyone else was beneath him in stature, Mudit never made an effort to get to know his classmates. He didn't even remember the names of some of his classmates who were introverts and didn't participate much in class.

On the other hand, Udit was a favorite of his classmates. Despite the fact that he himself was an average student, he was a kind person and never afraid of sharing knowledge about whatever new concept he had learnt of.

He was the person who would ensure that if any class-mate had missed any class for any reason, he would at least receive the notes. If any of his friends forgot his lunch, Udit would share his lunch with him/her. He was in the habit of appreciating his fellow beings and thanking them if he received any help from them. He was an icon of humility and helpfulness. He remembered the birth-day of each classmate by heart and never forgot to wish them. In fact, he had maintained a specific diary for this purpose where he maintained a list of these important dates. Other students in his peer group also reciprocated his kindness. Everyone appreciated his sense of co-opera-tion and the tendency to help anyone in need. He, as a result, was always surrounded by people.

During the course of time, both friends grew up, found employment, got married, and got busy with their own lives. Because of his good grades and sharp brain, Mudit found a better job than Udit, but Udit never felt envious of his friend.

Mudit now immersed himself in his work. Desperate to grow faster than everyone else, he spent most of his time in office and hardly had any time for his family. School friends anyways were long forgotten. The only school friend he was in touch with was Udit, and that too only because Udit himself made the effort and called Mudit. Not only Mudit, Udit was in fact in touch with all his classmates from school. In due time, many of their school friends had worked hard and scaled great heights. Mudit was oblivious of them but Udit was aware of what each of these friends was doing. All his friends too respected Udit for his concern and continuous efforts to keep in touch with them.

Mudit didn't realize this, but because he hardly had any time for leisure and because he hardly had any friends, he had started developing signs of stress. He wasn't even that close to his wife so never shared any of his worries with her. His health deteriorated and he could not work as efficiently as he used to. His confidence had come crashing down and this did not go unnoticed. He was scolded many times by his boss and once when he fumbled during a meeting with an important client, the Vice President of his company publicly humiliated him. This made his condition worse. His situation was now like that of someone caught in a whirlpool. His wife, his daughter, and his parents were very worried for him. However, they had never felt too comfortable talking to him, and on his part, he didn't want to accept that he was in trouble, and, therefore, didn't speak to them. But his father was getting restless day by day. When he couldn't bear it anymore, he asked Mudit, "What is wrong? Is everything alright at work?" Avoiding looking his father in the eyes, Mudit replied tersely, "yes, of course." "You look worried and stressed all the time," his father insisted. "Papa, why do you keep thinking negative all the time? Everything is absolutely fine. Don't irritate me," Mudit replied and walked out.

His father, however, was not satisfied. So one day when he found out that Mudit is on leave, he decided to visit his son's office without telling him. However, when he reached the office, the receptionist refused to let him see the vice-president without prior appointment. He waited there for hours but could not convince the receptionist. The receptionist, who greeted everyone with a smile, had never got a smile back from Mudit. Instead, one day Mudit had scolded her in the presence of several people when she had transferred a wrong call to his desk. Therefore, the receptionist did not feel any sympathy for Mudit's father.

At the end of the day, Mudit's father left the office with a heavy heart. He was feeling very sad that his son, even after working in this office for years, had no standing among the staff. He was thinking about all this when he suddenly felt dizzy and fell down on the road outside the office. Many people gathered around him, and among them was Udit, who just happened to be passing by. He recognized the old gentleman as Mudit's father. Immediately, he hired an auto rickshaw and took Mudit's father to a doctor close by, where they learned that Mudit's father had narrowly escaped a heart attack.

As soon as Udit found out about the reason behind Mudit's father's illness, he decided to go and meet the vice-president himself. He went to the security guard first and enquired about the vice-president. The vice-president turned out to be one of their classmates. While in school, he was very shy and introverted, so Mudit had never noticed him and even till date had failed to recognize him. The vice-president had, on the other hand, recognized Mudit, but decided to stay quiet when Mudit did not show any sign of recognition

Udit politely asked the receptionist to inform the vice president that an old friend from his school is waiting for him. Upon learning the name of the visitor, the vice-president immediately asked her to send Udit in. When they were classmates, Udit was the only one who had tried to draw him out of his shyness, and the vice-president still remembered this gesture.

After talking about general things Udit discussed the problems that Mudit was facing with the Vice-President. He made the Vice-President understand what a valuable asset Mudit was to his company and how the company should also support him when he was going through a tough period. The Vice-President respected Udit's views and was able to appreciate his perspective. He decided to ease the work pressure off Mudit and give him some time to recuperate.

Mudit was surprised to see the change in his boss's attitude and upon enquiring about the reason, he came to know how Udit had talked to him on his behalf. He felt very grateful to Udit and also admired the fact that Udit hadn't done this for any selfish reasons. In fact, Udit hadn't even told him that he had helped him. Mudit was filled with respect for his childhood friend. He understood the value of compassion and empathy in human relationships.

Investing in relationships always pays off. We must learn to appreciate relationships without ever expecting anything in return. Relationships that are founded on the grounds of friendship, trust, respect, and regard for each other, are the ones that come to our rescue when we are feeling low. On the other hand, relationships that are formed on the basis of selfish desires never last long.

MAKE AN EFFORT

Healthy relationships can play an important role in times of dire need or when we are depressed because of any reason. Friendship provides us comfort, for we can be sure that our friends will always be there if we need them. Friendship usually develops spontaneously. We do not need to draw huge plans or strategies to make good friends, however we do need to make an effort. If we like someone, we need to invest some time in getting to know the person and in letting the other person know us to let friendship germinate. If your wavelengths match, two people who simply enjoy hanging out together may end up becoming lifelong friends. Developing and maintaining relationships takes time, but at the end it is all worth it.

Usually if two people are going to get along, the comradery is apparent in the first few interactions. However, this is not a rule. At times people who can't stand each other, end up becoming the best of friends. So while it is great to hang out with people you get along with, it is good to be polite with people you do not hit it off with, so that you do not block any future prospects of a great partnership.

Respect is the key to forming and maintaining relationships. How you treat your friends, family members, and everyone around you says a lot about you as a person. Think about it. When was the last time you had a heart-to-heart chat with your parents? When was the last time you called up a friend just to find out how he/she was doing in life? If you are in the habit of doing this, you value your relationships and actually spend time in nurturing them. Otherwise, you may not realize this but you are creating distance between yourself and the people you love.

IT IS NOT WHAT YOU SAY, BUT HOW YOU SAY IT

Our language is a mirror to our personality. What we speak may turn into actions, the result of which can be positive or negative. Rude and harsh words create bitterness that attracts negativity. Our words carry enormous weight. More than we think. They often impact people for decades.

Author Yehuda Berg says:

"Words have energy and power with the ability to help, to heal, to hinder, to hurt, to harm, to humiliate, and to humble."

Words can transform our childhood friend into a lifelong enemy. Wounds that are caused by physical injury heal with the passing of time, but those caused by words can stay raw for decades. Thoughtless words can ruin our oldest and closest relationship in no time.

Ask yourself this question – who would you rather be with? Someone who talks about negative things all the time, does not think twice before insulting others, uses unpleasant and derogatory language and never misses a chance to taunt someone? Or someone who is always respectful to the others, who is well-mannered even when he/she is offering criticism, who knows how to treat others with dignity, and who appreciates people for what they are capable of? Our guess is that you would rather hang out with the second kind of person.

Being polite and courteous doesn't mean that you have to be a pushover and agree to everything everyone says to you. It doesn't mean that you cannot be firm with your juniors. It doesn't even mean that you cannot discipline your children. You can do all of the above in a positive, constructive, and respectful tone. Consider the following scenario where two seniors are reprimanding their juniors for missed deadlines. The juniors in both the cases are fresh out of the college and have just started working.

Senior 1: "This way you will not last in this job for too long. I need to keep a closer watch on your work now. See me once every week and update me about the status of your tasks."

Senior 2: "I know you are new here, but I do expect you to keep me updated if you think you are going to miss a deadline. For the next few weeks, let's monitor the situation more closely. Please set a meeting with me once every week. We will try to resolve issues proactively."

Senior 1 wasn't rude, but his remarks showed that he lacked trust in the junior's abilities. The junior was new, he definitely needed guidance, but the senior's approach wasn't constructive. The junior will probably feel that the senior isn't on his side.

Senior 2, on the other hand, was firm and direct. He made it clear that he expected better from the junior. This indirectly also indicates that he has faith that the junior can do better.

This is positive criticism. It makes apparent to the junior that the senior is there to support him and that the senior has his best interest in mind. The junior may feel bad for some time, but if he is a reasonable person, he will try to learn from the situation.

You can see in the above example that one doesn't have to abuse someone to cause long-lasting harm; words that are spoken without consideration can do as much damage.

Just like thoughtless words can create issues where there weren't any, thoughtful words can diffuse a potentially explosive situation. We see such examples around us all the time. People who are admired by others because they are able to take a stand without making enemies or breaking hearts. There are people who know how to say 'no' without spoiling a relationship. The secret lies in how logical your stand is and how strongly you believe in it. If your arguments are logical and your reasons for saying 'no' reasonable and you put your thoughts in words and tone that convey to the other person that though you are saying 'no', your response is simply for that suggestion and not for the person himself/herself, you will probably not lose a friend. As long as while saying 'no', you make it clear that you are rejecting that particular suggestion and not the person on the whole, chances are the other person will understand and not hold it against you. At least not for too long, if you continue treating the person as a friends even after the incident.

Abraham Lincoln asked a very valid question:

"Do I not destroy my enemies when I make them my friends?"

It pays to think before we talk and choose proper words to turn difficult situations into our favor. When we understand the power of words and realize that we can choose what we think and speak, our lives can be transformed.

REMEMBER THOSE WHO WERE THERE FOR YOU

Think of the struggles you have been through in your life. Think about those who stood by you, held your hands, and showed you the way during those times. Try listing down these names. Initially you may come up with only a few names, but if you think really hard, recall the seemingly small struggles, the list will grow longer. Once you are done this, you will realize that you have a lot to be thankful for. And you will also realize that there are some people in your life who you need to treasure. Remember them and be there for them in their times of need.

Consider this example of a King who forgot to be thankful to those who were good to him. He learnt his lesson and had an opportunity to mend his ways.

The King and his Courtier

Once upon a time, there was a King who ruled a small kingdom on an Island. He was sovereign authority in himself. His words were a rule for all his subjects. He lived a lavish life in a very big royal palace, which was looked after by a brigade of servants and courtiers. He had everything he could wish for. However, he had one big flaw. He enjoyed bloodshed and as there were no wars in his kingdom, he often became cruel to his own subjects.

For smallest of mistakes, he awarded the most brutal punishments. His favorite was putting the offender in an enclosure with hungry hunting dogs and watching the person be devoured to bones.

The dogs that he employed for this terrible game were taken care of by two caretakers who had been instructed to keep them hungry for days before someone was scheduled to be killed by the dogs.

One day, one of his courtiers arrived late for his duty. This particular courtier was responsible for the upkeep of the personal attire of the King. The King, therefore, was kept waiting and was late in attending the royal court. This was treated as a grave mistake that attracted punishment. This courtier was in service of the king for the last twenty years and was very sincere, honest, hardworking and loyal to the King. However, the King was not in the habit of sparing anyone. Without taking into consideration, the courtier's past good record, the King ordered his soldiers to throw him in the cage of hungry dogs.

The courtier prayed and begged the King, "Oh, Lord! You are like God for all of us, have some mercy. I have served you wholeheartedly for two decades please forgive me and spare my life."

King was adamant; he didn't want to lose the chance of watching the most entertaining feat of a living man being torn into pieces by hungry dogs. He refused and ordered his soldiers to execute the penalty

The courtier again pleaded, "Oh King! You are our God and we cannot disobey your orders. But keeping in mind my children and family, kindly allow me ten days to arrange for their well-being."

King agreed to grant him 10 days and warned that no further time shall be allowed. The courtier thanked the God and went straight to meet the caretakers of the dogs. He pleaded with the caretakers to allow him to serve the dogs for ten days.

The Dog's caretakers laughed and said, "What will you gain by serving the very dogs that are soon going to tear apart your flesh bit by bit from every inch of your body?"

"You will not understand this," replied the courtier. However, the caretakers allowed the courtier his last wish.

During those ten days, the courtier took good care of all the dogs. He cleaned them, bathed them, fed them, and provided every type of comfort to all the dogs. He practically lived with the dogs, played with them, and even slept with them. He did this throughout the 10 days, including the last 2 days when the dogs were to be kept hungry. He took good care of them even when the dogs were irritable when they were hungry.

On the 11th day, the King's men dragged the courtier to the compound where the hungry dogs were struggling to break loose. The King took front seat and behind him sat his family members, other soldiers, and courtiers who were ordered to be present to watch the show.

The hands of accused courtier were tied, he was blindfolded and then thrown into the cage of hungry dogs. All of those present there had seen such shows earlier as well.

They knew that the moment a person is thrown into the cage all dogs pounce upon him like skilled hunters. They pull down their prey quickly and devour them with astonishing speed. A pack of ten dogs reduces a human body to scraps of skin and bone within 20 minutes. Everyone was anticipating the same kind of performance again.

But to their dismay, nothing like that happened. Instead, the hungry dogs stood still watching their prey. They looked confused. A moment later the dogs started sniffing courtier and started pulling at the rope that tied his hands. Two dogs started licking the courtier and almost all were wagging their tales wildly as if they were meeting a long-lost friend.

The king was angry and furious to see his most entertaining sport spoiled. Instead of killing the man the dogs were showering him with love. He asked the courtier what he had done to all the dogs.

His reply was simple, "Oh King! I have served these dogs only for ten days and they haven't forgotten what I did for them. But you, who are a human being and a great King, forgot what I did for you for the last 20 years."

This response touched the King. If animals could be thankful to people who had served them, he, a human being and a king, had to be better. This little incident taught the King a very important lesson. He abolished the cruel punishment and personally thanked the courtier who had shown him the right way.

Swami Vivekanand has also spoken about this great trait. This is what he has said:

Who is helping you, don't forget them.
Who is loving you, don't hate them.
Who is believing you, don't Cheat them.

Stay Successful

Success means different things to different people. While for some people, success is when they become the President of the US, for other people, success is when they are able to fulfil their commitments in time. But success, however big or small, comes with its own baggage. Once you are successful, people's expectations from you increase. They trust you with bigger and better things and expect you to succeed. The stakes are higher. The responsibility is bigger. So it is essential that you are aware of this change in position and know how to cope with it. This will help you stay successful.

Following are some of things that you should be aware of and keep in mind once you have started achieving success:

1. DON'T LET SUCCESS GO TO YOUR HEAD

Successes, even small ones, are tricky to handle. It is easy to forget yourself and your roots in the wake of success. It is very easy to get carried away. Here's an example. Anand had just been hired by an insurance firm. It was his first quarter there and his manager had set targets for him. These targets were slightly lower than what he had set for more experienced employees, but were by no means easy to achieve. Anand worked hard throughout the quarter and achieved his target before the deadline. His joy knew no bounds. His boss congratulated him and set his target at par with the rest of his colleagues for the next quarter.

This was a huge deal. Never in the history of the company had a freshman been treated at par with experienced employees so early on in his/her career. Anand celebrated with his family and friends. He spent his incentive on buying clothes for himself. He was indeed very happy.

When the next quarter started, Anand was confident that he could achieve the targets. During his first quarter, he had made some excellent contacts in corporates and they had promised him good business. So he relaxed. When he should have been in the field, trying to find more prospects, he went out for lunches with his college friends. When he should have started early for work, he slept till late. By the time Anand decided that he should now start working towards his target, half of the quarter was already over. He was still not worried. He called up his contacts. Some of them informed him that they had postponed their decisions while others told him that since he hadn't called them up earlier, they had purchased insurance from another company. Now Anand was worried. He tried to contact his friends and family members and tried to convince them to buy insurance, but they said that they needed time to think. By the time the quarter ended, Anand had not even achieved half of his target. He was disheartened, but it was now too late. Anand's boss too realized his mistake and again lowered Anand's target. This was a big blow for Anand. Had he tried a little harder, had he not got carried away by his success in the first quarter, he could have surely achieved this new target. He decided to work hard consistently so that he could stay successful always.

2. REMEMBER YOUR GUIDING VALUES

The pressure to stay successful can be very tough to handle. And this is why it is so tough to be the Prime Minister of a country or the team captain of a popular sport. People expect the best from you always and they are not ready to settle for anything less. Captains of our cricket teams have had fans protesting outside their homes, burning their effigies when they lost a tournament. You can imagine the amount of pressure these leaders need to handle. Similarly, the top performers in a corporate, the highest scorers in a class are also under tremendous pressure. In such a scenario, it can be very tempting to take a route that is against your guiding principles, if at any time you feel that you cannot keep up your performance. And this is the biggest test. While it is easy to give in to temptation, it is difficult to persevere on your straight path. However, once you take a step in the wrong direction, it is very difficult to turn back. You may find yourself in a vortex, giving in to temptation after temptation till you do not recognize yourself anymore. If this is something you do not want to do, make all your decisions with your guiding principles in sight. This way you may not rise exponentially, but you will sleep easy at night.

3. BE COMPASSIONATE TO OTHERS

You are now successful and people around you are aware of how good you are with what you do. People love you and look up to you. But success is weird in this regard too.

Michelle Obama, First Lady of the US, put this very aptly in her speech at the Democratic National Convention in Charlotte, North Carolina, US. She said, "Being President doesn't change who you are, it reveals who you are." Your success too will do the same. It will reveal who you are as a person. If after you are successful, you are not compassionate to those who fail or are yet to achieve their share of success, it will reveal a very ugly side of you. Once you are successful, remember that there was a time when you too were struggling. That you too made mistakes. That you can still make mistakes. Be compassionate to those who make mistakes. Try to make it slightly easy for them. Don't mock them for their failure, nor cite their examples to others. Besides being a very mean thing to do, it is also the easiest way to lose friends. And by this we do not mean only those who you mock, but also those who see you mocking others. They will remember who not to trust in future.

4. REMEMBER THE LESSONS THAT YOU LEARNT

Once you are on the other side of success, it is easy to forget your journey towards it. It is easy to forget the lessons you learnt with so much difficulty. It is easy to forget what it took to reach where you are. And with these lessons forgotten, your success loses its worth. It is just a milestone. You are none the wiser for achieving it. So when you are successful, make an effort to remember those lessons. Making the same mistakes again to learn the very same lessons is in no way a smart move.

5. REMEMBER THOSE WHO WERE WITH YOU WHEN YOU WERE STRUGGLING

So many Bollywood movies have been made on this theme. *Shree 420* (1955), *Fashion* (2008), and *Luck By Chance* (2009) are just some of them. All of them tell the story of an individual coming from a humble background and after a brief struggle achieving success. Invariably, upon achieving success, these individuals forget those who supported them during their struggle and the result is for everyone to see. In real world, things are not so dramatic. But heartbreak, bitterness, and loss of trust are the same. So whenever you achieve success, remember those who were with you in tough times, keep in touch with them, and be there for them when they need you.

6. REMEMBER THAT TIMES CHANGE

Remember the example of Anand in point 1? He was successful in one quarter, but in the very next quarter, success evaded him. This is bound to happen sometime or the other. Even if you have gotten used to succeeding every time you set a goal for yourself, rest assured that there will still be some instances in future where you may not be able to achieve the desired results. While we do not want to promote negative thinking, it is best to be aware of this. It will help you stay grounded in the instance of success.

7. HELP THOSE WHO NEED HAND-HOLDING

When you see someone struggling to achieve their goal, be generous with help. It doesn't have to be someone junior to you in hierarchy. However, it is important to be careful even when offering help. Do not approach in a superior tone. Don't assume that you will be able to help. It may be that the problem is beyond your capabilities. Ask them what they are struggling with. Ask them if they need any help and whether it is okay with them if you offer suggestions. Unsolicited advice can easily sound condescending.

8. STAY OPEN TO LEARNING FROM OTHERS

Just like you feel that other people can learn a lot from you, you too can learn a lot from them. And not only from those who are more experienced, more successful than you. You can learn valuable lessons from people who are younger, less experienced, less intellectual, less educated than you. Consider the example of a very successful business man who happens to have tea at a local *chai-wala*.

The Businessman and the Chai-wala
A successful businessman is contemplating marrying his daughter off as soon as she finishes her college. She doesn't

need to have a career. He is, of course, going to find a groom who is a successful businessman himself. Deep in his thoughts, he gestures to the chai wala for a cup of tea. The chai wala is in the habit if talking to all his clients. He doesn't ask them questions, just shares what is going on in his mind. Incidentally, he too has been thinking of his daughter who is just about to complete graduation. "She says she wants to become a professor," he confides in the businessman who is sipping slowly on his tea. "And what are you going to do about it?" asks the businessman. "What can I do about this, saab? I can only offer my blessings. She says she will apply for scholarship. But even if she doesn't get a scholarship, I will gladly fund her education." "But why? Tomorrow you need to marry her off. You will need money for that too. Why not save the money and marry her off now? Her in-laws, if they want, will let her study?" The chai wala smiled and said, "Saab, there is no way to predict future. Who knows what kind of people her in-laws would be? Marriage may not last, but education and qualification will never leave her. I don't want her to be dependent on anyone ever. This is the only way to ensure her happiness." The businessman was moved by this man's thinking. He felt a little ashamed of his own narrow vision. He decided that upon reaching home, he would ask his daughter what she wants to do next and accordingly plan for the future.

So you can see that one needs to be humble and only then can one hope to learn from the others, especially from those junior to you. In humility lies the real success.

9. DON'T FEAR FAILURE

Success and failure are part of life. None of these should excite or worry you too much. A truly successful individual is the one who doesn't fail with failure. Whenever you fail to achieve a goal, remember that it is in that particular task that you have failed. You are not a failure. There is difference in both. Remember, it is possible to fall down from any pedestal and it is possible to bounce back from any failure, as long as you do not admit defeat. In case of failure, stay put, persevere, and some door or the other will open for you.

10. REMEMBER YOUR BIG DREAM

While battling this cycle of success and failure, don't lose sight of your ultimate dream. Go after it as relentlessly as you did for your goal. Keep on working towards it. Achieving your goal is just a milestone, your dream is your destination. Remember that it is up to you to achieve it. If you give up on it or forget it because of temporary success, you are giving up on an opportunity to create history, to actually make a difference. Cherish your dream. Celebrate your goals, but worship your dream. It is sacred.

If you follow these 10 rules after achieving success, you can be sure that you will have no regrets in your life and there is no bigger blessing than this. Now go on, achieve your dream. It will be priceless.

Student's Encyclopedia of
General Knowledge
by Dr. Ruth Premi

Price	:	Rs. 175
Pages	:	96
Size	:	9.5x7.25 inches
Binding	:	Paperback
Language	:	English
Subject	:	Children's Books/GK
ISBN	:	9789380914190

National Bestseller

OVER 40,000 COPIES SOLD

This encyclopedia is the best source of information and reference in a single volume, particularly for students of classes III to VIII. It provides the best of GK to its readers. Every piece of information is authentic—culled together from several areas of knowledge ranging from encyclopedias, fact books, year books, official government releases, internet and other reliable sources—and verified for accuracy.

Salient Features:

»   The best reference book for students, teachers and parents
»   Includes the most up-to-date facts & figures
»   Alphabetical order of entries in each chapter
»   'Believe It or Not' boxes contain over 100 amazing facts
»   Quiz at the end contains 200 important questions
»   Over 100 lavish & spectacular illustrations
»   Index contains around 200 direct & cross entries

TOP 10 BOOKS OF GENERAL PRESS

» Relativity by Albert Einstein, Rs 295
Science/Physics, ISBN : 9789380914220

» The Diary of a Young Girl by Anne Frank, Rs 275
Autobiography/Memoir, ISBN : 9789380914312

» The Autobiography of Benjamin Franklin, Rs 295
Autobiography/Memoir, ISBN : 9788190276689

» Siddhartha by Hermann Hesse, Rs 225
Literature & Fiction/Classic, ISBN : 9789380914145

» Student's Encyclopedia of General Knowledge, Rs 175
Children's Non-Fiction/GK, ISBN : 9789380914190

» The Gita Way by Shweta and Santosh, Rs 250
Religion/Hindu, ISBN : 9789380914879

» Love Happens only Once by Rochak Bhatnagar, Rs 175
Literature & Fiction/Romance, ISBN : 9789380914183

» One Life, One Love by Rochak Bhatnagar, Rs 175
Literature & Fiction/Romance, ISBN : 9789380914350

» The Girl I Last Loved by Smita Kaushik, Rs 175
Literature & Fiction/Romance, ISBN : 9789380914244

» Because…Every Raindrop is a Hope by Sankalp Kohli, Rs 175
Literature & Fiction/Romance, ISBN : 9789380914435

74272781R00124

Made in the USA
San Bernardino, CA
14 April 2018